Why Should I Care?

Lessons from the Holocaust

**(WITH A CONCISE
HISTORY OF THE HOLOCAUST)**

Jeanette Friedman
&
David Gold

Foreword
by Dr. Michael Berenbaum

The Wordsmithy, LLC
2009

ISBN 978-1-935110-03-3

Why Should I Care? Lessons from the Holocaust school edition: published by The Wordsmithy, LLC.

First edition April 2009
Second Edition (revised) May 2009
Third Edition (revised) June 2009

Trade paperback edition, *The Snake Made Me Do It*, published by Gihon River Press, New York.

We dedicate this book to our parents.

Peska and Volvie Friedman

&

Helen and Vilmos Gold

They suffered through the Holocaust
and lost families and children.
After liberation, they chose to come to America
to realize their dreams of rebuilding their families
and their faith in humanity.

They succeeded.

Acknowledgments

Why Should I Care? Lessons from the Holocaust is a work of passion and dedication that could never have been written in a vacuum. Just as it takes a village to raise a child, it took many people who helped us in many different ways to bring this book to press.

First we want to thank our families. Our spouses and children, siblings and grandchildren were our harshest critics, and told us exactly what they thought right to our faces and on googletalk. We wanted to know why what we were trying to say wasn't working and would bug them until they said we'd gotten it right. They are Jeanette's husband, Philip, her son Daniel Sieradski, daughters Aviva Sieradski and L'via Wiesinger, and her grandsons Zevi and Akiva Weisinger. David's wife, Debbie Gold, was there with us as we honed the text, as were his children Elie, Tamar, Dov, Aryeh and Daniel, and David's sisters, Malka and Sharon.

Thinkers and scholars, theologians and historians, survivors, editors and friends inspired us and taught us how to look at the material and how to think about it. A special thanks to Professor Yehuda Bauer, whose insightful comments made us address issues that, we believe, have added to the relevance of this work.

Two rabbis deserve top billing. Dr. Michael Berenbaum's and Rabbi Jack Bemporad's teachings and insights have profoundly influenced the philosophy and ideas at the heart of this book. Michael double and triple checked our history, and Jack's ideas and methodologies shaped our message. Dr. Alex Grobman was a major source for us on the two aspects of Holocaust denial.

Fred Zeidman, Paul Shapiro, and Ellen Blalock at the United States Holocaust Memorial Museum offered encouragement and advice. Colleen Tambuscio, head of the Council of Holocaust Educators, was the teacher who told us that what we had was just what she was looking for. Especially the urls! (links to websites).

Sarah K. Steiner, Robin Katz, and Maxine Dovere read and re-read the manuscript, catching grammatical errors and typos, letting us know when sentences didn't seem to make sense, and cautioning us when we sounded too preachy.

Ernest W. Michel, Peska Friedman, Menachem Rosensaft, Roman Kent, Max and Hanne Liebmann, Mahli Lieblich, Lea Wolnitz and David Kelsey contributed stories, ideas and criticism.

Steve Feuer at Gihon River Press pushed us to finish the book and convinced us it was marketable. Skip McWilliams of Teacher's Discovery told us it was needed, and Dr. Alan Willis at Socialstudies.com encouraged us to get it done in time for his catalogue deadline.

Many more of our friends looked over the manuscript, talked it up and told us to keep at it. We wish we could name everyone, and hope that those we left out will forgive us.
Lastly, we want to thank Larry Page and Sergey Brin for inventing Google. They saved us hundreds of dollars in phone bills and gasoline, while allowing ten people to say what they wanted to say, all at the same time. They also saved us hundreds upon hundreds of hours in research time, and

made it possible to find the best websites that helped us
make our lessons clear.

Any errors in this book are our responsibility. Please let us
know if you find any so we can fix them in the next edition.

Jeanette Friedman
New Milford, NJ

David Gold
Wesley Hill, NY

April 2009

TABLE of CONTENTS

*A*n accountable person is not a victim and doesn't shift blame or claim credit for the work of others. He considers the likely consequences of his behavior and associations. He recognizes the common complicity in the triumph of evil when nothing is done to stop it. He leads by example.

Michael S. Josephson
Making Ethical Decisions
Josephson Institute of Ethics
San Mateo, CA

Foreword

It is now commonly accepted wisdom that the Holocaust is one of the defining events of 20th century humanity. It tells us much about the dark side of culture and civilization, of institutions, government and society—and is an event that is central to all discussions of values.

In my own work I have argued that the Holocaust is the "negative absolute" in a world of relativism. In a world that sees most values as relative and most claims as contextual, the Holocaust is understood as the product of its time and place but not of all times and all places. In a world where we do not know for sure or for long what is good and what is bad, we know for sure—and for long—that the Holocaust was evil. And thus, it has become the touchstone of values.

This book, *Why Should I Care? Lessons from the Holocaust*, undertakes the very important task of translating a historical event into value terms that are applicable to students. It applies to their lives today in classrooms and at home, in school yards and in playgrounds, in the malls and on the Internet—not in the abstract world of values, but in the concrete places where students spend their time and expend their energy. Such is the virtue of this work, but also its limitation.

Were a book on the Holocaust to be read by physicians, they would have to deal with the role of doctors. Nazi doctors administered cruel and scientifically reckless experiments on patients who had no choice but to be guinea pigs – with no consent, no anesthesia. One would also have to examine the role of science that allowed doctors, ordinarily committed to saving the lives of their patients, to consign handicapped patients or the incurably ill to death. It was easier that way.

Were a book on the Holocaust to be read by lawyers, it would have to deal with the role of law. Not law as the defender of rights and liberties, but as the instrument by which a government defines, isolates and murders an entire population – and then confiscates and redistributes its property. It would have to show why almost half of the 15 men gathered at the 1942 Wannsee Conference were lawyers and why no one objected when the murder of the Jews, "The Final Solution to the Jewish Problem," was announced and its planning coordinated. It would have to explain how a democracy became a totalitarian state – all under the rule of law. How can law be detached from values, from the protection of all citizens of the state, from the equality of all people?

Were a book about the Holocaust intended for engineers or architects, it would have to ask how men and women who create such beauty could – without objection – also design death camps complete with gas chambers and crematoria.

Were a book about the Holocaust intended for clergy, it would be forced to address why certain religious teachings were used to rescue Jews from all but certain death. It would need to examine why and how other teachings, of the same faith and tradition, from the same Scripture, were used to condemn Jews to their deaths. How can religion, an instrument that celebrates the divine within each of us, become a means of claiming that we alone have a monopoly on truth? How can it instill the certitude to proclaim that ours is the only path, the only way?

Were such a book intended for government officials, it would have to ask how the tools of government can be used to protect human decency, to enlarge human responsibility, to embrace human diversity. How could those same tools be used to imprison and murder those the government deems expendable?

If such a work were written for teachers and not their students, it would ask how we can teach you values so that human dignity is preserved, human values embraced. Is school a place to sensitize students to their humanity and responsibilities? Or is it a desensitizing institution that invites discrimination and turns students against each other?

Every individual, in any profession, must confront the questions the Holocaust raises for the humanity we share in common. The answers drive the choices we make as to how we earn our livings and the ways we live our lives.

Why Should I Care? asks such questions of you, the students, at this stage in your lives—before you have chosen careers, before you have entered adulthood. Now there is still time to shape your character—to learn what is important about the past and urgent about the future. You need to know history, but you also need to feel called upon to change the path of history.

We once thought that the age of genocide was over. But we live in a world in which each generation experiences genocide; Cambodia, Biafra, the former Yugoslavia, Rwanda and Darfur are places of infamy.

Still, we dare not despair and we dare not give up. We will not abandon the naïve but all important hope that if you study the past, you can be energized to do better for the future.

I belong to a unique group of men and women who probe the ashes of the murdered not merely to remember the dead and pay homage to their memory. I want to find something

from the horror of their deaths and the evil of their murders that can speak to our common humanity and deepen
our commitment to human rights. The authors of this work,
Jeanette Friedman and David Gold, share that commitment.
They want to share it with you. They want you to be their
partners in this all important enterprise.

We study this intolerance to teach tolerance. We explore
this inhumanity to teach humanity. We examine an event
that turned students and adults against one another so we
can find a way to turn you toward one another. The work
that we have bequeathed to you requires it. Let's hope the
world you shape will be better for it.

Michael Berenbaum,
Professor of Jewish Studies
Director, Sigi Ziering Institute: Exploring the Ethical and Reli-
gious Implications of the Holocaust
American Jewish University, Los Angeles, California
Former Project Director of the creation of the USHMM

INTRODUCTION

SINCE 1900 MORE THAN 100 MILLION PEOPLE HAVE BEEN MURDERED BY GOVERNMENTS, HALF OF THEM IN GENOCIDES
(See Epilogue)

IMAGINE you are at home. You are playing video games late at night when suddenly you hear trucks rumbling down the street. Gunshots and screams fill the air. You look out your window and see men in uniforms holding rifles and pushing your neighbors and friends into the trucks or into lines and marching them out of sight, never to be seen again. Some of your neighbors are lying on the sidewalk, collapsed in pools of blood.

How and why did this happen?
How could this happen?
Was there a way to stop it?

WHAT COULD YOU HAVE DONE
TO STOP IT?

The nonpragmatic character of the genocide of the Jews is one of the elements that differentiate it from other genocides. Other elements were the totality, that is, the desire to annihilate every single Jew defined as such by the Nazis; the universality, namely the idea, developed in stages, that Jews everywhere should be treated the same way that they were being treated in Nazi Europe; and the fact that special industrial enterprises were set up, in the death camps, for the purpose of producing (Jewish) corpses — an unprecedented historical fact.

Yehuda Bauer
"Reviewing the Holocaust
Anew in Multiple Contexts"
Jerusalem Center for Public Affairs, April 2009

WHAT IS THE HOLOCAUST?

A holocaust, with a small "h," means "a fiery sacrifice." In the 1950s, the word Holocaust, with a capital H, was introduced to describe a specific genocide. In Hebrew, it is called the *Shoah*. This 1933-1945 genocide was the systematic state-sponsored murder of millions of Jews in Europe by the Germans and their collaborators.

The political party that ran the government at that time was called the National Socialist Party—the Nazis. Adolf Hitler—an avowed antisemite and racist—was its leader. His followers committed genocide to realize the dream of a master race that would rule the world.

History has proven that genocide can happen anywhere when a group of people is targeted by another more powerful group for any reason—religion, ethnicity, sex, economics, skin color, country of origin, political ideology or other excuse.

WHY WAS THE HOLOCAUST DIFFERENT?

1. It was unprecedented. No government had ever targeted every single member of a specific group for extinction. During the Holocaust Jews were targeted just because they were born Jewish or had Jewish grandparents.

2. The Holocaust was conceived by one of the most "civilized" and technologically advanced of nations that

created an ideology based on lies about another group of
people. These concepts were then used to convince the
Germans that the death of every single Jew would be their
salvation.

3. Most genocide is limited to a specific geographical area. In
this instance, however, Jews the world over were targeted by
the Nazis. Had the Nazis conquered Great Britain, the U.S.S.R
and the United States, Jews there would have been murdered
just as commitedly as in Nazi-occupied Europe.

4. Most genocide takes place for seemingly "practical"
considerations—like nationalism, expansion of land and
acquisition of resources. But there was no "rational"
reason for targeting the Jews. The Jews had no army and
no territory. Only a handful were very wealthy, and they
certainly had no power. But they did have Jewish "blood"—a
Nazi term. Jewish "blood" was the enemy, ironic since we
know blood transfusions routinely take place between
people of all races!

5. The Holocaust was unprecedented in scope, scale and
duration. It covered the world from June 22, 1941 until May
8, 1945, a four-year period of industrialized mass murder.

"WHY SHOULD I CARE?"

Once a group is targeted—it could even be your group—
the propaganda machine is put into motion to create
fear of that group in the general population. Fear then turns
into hatred directed at the targeted group and marks the
beginning of their dehumanization and destruction.

Words, images and song are then used to describe the group
with degrading names; lies are told about their behavior and
culture. They are portrayed as troublemakers and threats
to personal and state security. They are held accountable
for national failures, financial and otherwise, that they did
not cause.

As the controlling power exhorts people to violence, anything can happen. History has shown that if you, your family and friends are members of a singled out entity, you will become targets of hate, discrimination and, eventually victims of genocide.

HOW DOES GENOCIDE SUCCEED?

Genocide can only succeed when neighbors begin to fear and hate their neighbors or stand idly by as their neighbors are persecuted. This happened in Turkey in 1915 when Ottoman Turks attacked their Armenian neighbors; in the 1970s, when Pol Pot's Communist regime murdered some 2 million people in Cambodia; in 1990 and 1999 in the Balkans, when Christians attacked Muslims; in 1994 in Rwanda, when Hutus attacked Tutsis, and in Darfur, where, since 2003, Arab Sudanese Muslims have attacked African Anime Black Muslims in the south.

HOW DO YOU PREVENT GENOCIDE?

The only way to prevent this type of behavior is by changing the ways people think about each other, the ways we think about ourselves, and the ways we treat each other.

The Holocaust teaches us that we must fight racism and hatred, because if we don't, evil will flourish. We are responsible and accountable for our actions. And we are particularly accountable if we remain silent in the face of injustice and the killing of innocents and innocence.

❧

If I am not for myself, then who will be for me?
And if I am only for myself, then what am I?
And if not now, when?

Hillel
Ethics of the Fathers, **1:14**

❧

Fear breeds anger.
Anger breeds hate.
Hate breeds suffering.

Yoda
Jedi Warrior, *Star Wars*

❧

CHAPTER ONE

SILENCE = DEATH

ഔഃ

In Germany, they came first for the Communists, and I didn't speak up because I wasn't a Communist. Then they came for the trade unionists, and I didn't speak up because I wasn't a trade unionist. Then they came for the Jews and I didn't speak up because I wasn't a Jew. Then they came for me, and by that time, no one was left to speak up.

Pastor Martin Niemöller
German anti-Nazi theologian and Lutheran pastor,
imprisoned in Sachsenhausen and Dachau from 1937-1945
(There are many versions of this quote; this one is considered the most accurate.)

How much responsibility do you bear for the ill uses others might make of your ideas? Almost as much as the responsibility you bear if you fail to speak your ideas, when they might have made a difference in the world.

Orson Scott Card
Empire

Look outside the window
there's a woman being grabbed
They've dragged her to the bushes
and now she's being stabbed.
Maybe we should call the cops and try to stop the pain.
But Monopoly is so much fun
I'd hate to blow the game.
And I guess it wouldn't interest anybody —
outside of a small circle of friends

Phil Ochs, 1964
"Outside a Small Circle of Friends"

The expression Silence=Death gained currency in the 1980s when the AIDS epidemic ripped through gay communities. This equation holds true whenever people remain silent while others are being hurt, harmed or persecuted.

In 1964, Kitty Genovese was stabbed to death in her own neighborhood in Queens, New York. The song above is about her. She died because her neighbors did not care enough to call for help. Thirty-eight law-abiding citizens watched her attacker kill her from their windows but did not want to get involved. Not one of them called the police, and the 28-year-old woman bled to death on the street while crying, "I'm dying! I'm dying!"

The murderer then climbed into his car and drove away. Years later, he confessed to her brutal murder after being arrested for a different crime.[1]

Whether it's a single person walking down the street being mugged, bullied, knifed or shot, or a group of people being killed in another country, do not be complacent.

**Do not be an apathetic bystander.
Speak out.
Pursue justice.
Get involved.**

**Warning!
These actions can sometimes be
hazardous to your health.**

LIVIU LIBRESCU

Dr. Liviu Librescu, 76, was an aeronautical engineer and university professor who survived the concentration camps in the Eastern European area of Transnistria. During a shooting spree by a crazed student at Virginia Tech University, he protected his students by blocking the doorway to the classroom with his body while telling them to flee. Students opened windows and jumped, but the professor was shot and killed. Ironically, the shooting took place on April 16, 2007 — on Yom HaShoah, the Jewish observance of Holocaust Memorial Day. He will always be remembered as a hero.

WOMEN SHOUT OUT

The Rosenstrasse Protest in Berlin, Germany began on February 27, 1943. At that time millions of Jews were being put through the Nazi death machine. The Nazis rounded up the last 10,000 Jews of Berlin, including 1,800 Jewish men married to Christian women. Approximately 8,000 men were deported. Of the 1,800 Jewish husbands, 25 were sent to Auschwitz, the rest kept in Berlin.

But suddenly, the Nazis found themselves confronted with spontaneous protests. First there were protests in Central Berlin, in front of Nazi propaganda headquarters. For a week demands were made for the men's release. Led by their families and accompanied by friends, the protests started with a small group but rapidly grew until approximately 6,000 protestors came forward over the course of the demonstrations.[2]

Though threatened by German soldiers with machine guns, the protestors stood firm. To avoid a public relations disaster, Joseph Goebbels, Reich Minister of Public Enlightenment and Propaganda, told the Gestapo to release the prisoners and return the 25 men sent to Auschwitz. The 1,800 husbands went back to their wives and almost all of them survived the war.

ZACHOR! REMEMBER!

The watchword of the survivors of the Holocaust and their descendants is "*Zachor!*" Remember! Because human history repeats itself, they know that knowledge of the past helps us to recognize those factors that are potentially dangerous and affords us an opportunity to stop the madness.

The experience of the Rosenstrasse women is an example. They showed that we can speak up to those in power and prevail. We need courage, we need numbers, and we need to remember that we have the natural right to speak out. Just days before he invaded Poland, Hitler said, "Who after all, speaks today of the annihilation of the Armenians?" [On April 24, 1915, Ottoman authorities began the extermination of resident Armenians with the arrest of some 250 intellectuals and community leaders in Constantinople. "By the end of 1915 three-fourths of the Ottoman Armenians were extinct."[3]] Hitler realized that history is yesterday's news and quickly forgotten. He did not add that even if genocide is remembered, governments will do what is politically expedient first—even if it costs innocent lives.

The only possible way to stop genocide is for individuals to come together to take action and convince their governments to do the right thing. For example, American public protest during the 1990's wars in the Balkans convinced the U.S. to stop the genocide—first with bombs and then through negotiation: the Dayton Accords. Protest may not have overnight results, but it is our responsibility to speak out until evil is thwarted.

TRUTHINESS

Truthiness is an expression invented in 2005 by Stephen Colbert, star of a satirical political TV show, *The Colbert Report*. The word was introduced in the pilot episode and added to the Merriam-Webster dictionary in 2006. It was also voted "word of the year." It implies that people believe things based on intuition, "heart," and "gut feelings" without regard to evidence, logic, intellectual examination, or the facts of an issue. Hitler and his propaganda minister, Joseph Goebbels, already understood the concept years before and utilized it to advance their agenda. (Today the same tactics are used by radical Islamists to spread lies and hatred toward Christians, Americans, Jews, Bahais and others who are not of the Islamic faith. These radicals also kill people of their own religion who profess traditions or political views that are different from their own.)

We tend to believe whatever we read, see and hear, especially if it's on television news reports or in the newspapers—even more so when made at a presidential press conference. How can you know what is the truth? Governments push their own platforms or reasons to go to war; reporters have their own agendas and try to pass political messages off as "news." They sometimes even lie. When individuals or governments have their own agenda, they can manipulate "facts" to tell a non-factual story.

For example, on September 30, 2000, the *New York Times*

published a front page story marking the second day of the Intifada, the war that continues between Israel and the Palestinians. The story included a photo of what seemed to be an Israeli police officer beating a Palestinian on the Temple Mount. The message it sent was that the Israelis were brutal and that the Palestinian man was an innocent victim. In fact, the actual story was the opposite of what the photo showed.

The wounded man was Tuvia Grossman, an American Jew from Chicago who was attacked by Palestinian rock throwers. The police officer was trying to protect him from a Palestinian mob, not on the Temple Mount, as identified by the *Times,* but in an Arab neighborhood in Jerusalem. On October 7, 2000 the *Times* printed a full retraction—but the public relations damage to Israel had already been done.

In another instance, during the war between Israel and Lebanon in 2006, news services like Reuters used photographs taken by purportedly unbiased sources that depicted vicious Israeli aerial attacks. Videos were staged to generate public opinion against Israel. One photographer "Photoshopped" images of smoke above Beirut to make the damage look worse than it was. Later, Reuters had to disavow the photograph and set up procedures to prevent further photo fraud.

In yet another instance, President Mahmoud Ahmadinejad said Iran was developing a missile arsenal that would allow it to attack Israel and Europe. When it started testing missiles, Iran sent out government photographs of those tests. The photos, produced by the Iranian government and released through *Agence France-Presse,* show that at least one missile was added to the row. It is clear in the photograph that the dust kicked up by the launch of one missile is identical to the one right next to it, a task once again accomplished through the use of Photoshop. As usual, the *New York Times* and other major newspapers ran the story on their front pages without a careful examination. They were duped again. *The Lede*, The

Times' blog, ran a full analysis of the retouched photo on December 6, 2008.*

---

*See http://thelede.blogs.nytimes.com/2008/07/10/in-an-iranian-image-a-missile-too-many/?scp=4&sq=iran%20rockets%20photo%20dec%206&st=cse. Also, see chapter links on www.whyshouldicareontheweb.com.

Common people more readily fall victim to the big lie than the small lie, since they themselves often tell small lies in little matters but would be ashamed to resort to large-scale falsehoods.

Adolf Hitler
Mein Kampf

All the common people want is to be left alone. All the ordinary soldier wants is to collect his pay and not get killed. That's why the great forces of history can be manipulated by astonishingly small groups of determined people.

Orson Scott Card
Empire

If we could raise one generation with unconditional love, there would be no Hitlers. We need to teach the next generation of children from Day One that they are responsible for their lives. Mankind's greatest gift, also its greatest curse, is that we have free choice. We can make our choices built from love or from fear.

Dr. Elisabeth Kubler-Ross

CHAPTER TWO

THE SNAKE MADE ME DO IT

We must uphold the principle of only having carried out orders…We must stick to that principle if we are to create a more or less effective defence.[1]

General-Lieutenant Ferdinand Heim
incarcerated by the British after World War II,
while waiting to be tried as a war criminal.[1]

A MORALITY TALE IN THE GARDEN OF EDEN

There is a universal message in many Bible stories. The Garden of Eden story for example, goes way beyond religion to speak about acts and their consequences.

In the Garden of Eden Adam and Eve had only one condition to meet in order to live in perfection without responsibilities: They could not eat from the Tree of Knowledge. According to the story, the snake came along and challenged Eve with a question he knew was loaded. "Did God say, 'You shall not eat of any tree in the Garden?'"[2]

The snake spun the truth just enough to capture Eve's attention. Eve told the snake he was wrong; she and Adam could eat from any tree except the Tree of Knowledge. She also told the snake that eating the fruit would cause her death and added spin of her own—that even touching the tree would get her killed.

But the snake told her she would not die. Eating the fruit would make her like God, knowing the difference between good and evil.

Eve was tempted by the potential power offered by the fruit and ate it, sharing it with Adam. Then the story says their eyes were opened. They became self-aware. They understood, suddenly, that actions have consequences.

Suffering from the world's first manifestation of guilt, they covered their nakedness with fig leaves and hid.

God came calling in the Garden and asked Adam where he was—as if God did not know that he and Eve were hiding in the bushes. What God was really doing was waiting for an apology and He asked, "Who told you that you were naked?" The only way they could have known was because they had eaten from the Tree of Knowledge, and so God asked: "Did you eat from the tree I commanded you not to eat [from]?"[3] In other words, God was asking, "How do you know enough to feel so guilty?"

THE WORLD'S FIRST VICTIM

When confronted, Adam turned himself into the world's first victim. Instead of saying, "Sorry, I did the wrong thing. I ate from the tree you asked us not to eat from, and I am very sorry," he pointed to Eve and told God that "that" woman, God's gift to him, forced him to eat the fruit. In other words, he passed the buck. Adam didn't take responsibility for what he did. He said he was just following his wife's orders. Eve said "Eat." Adam ate.

When confronted, Eve did not give an excuse but immediately said, "The snake duped me, and I ate." In doing so, she also passed the buck.

Did the snake make them do it? No. They ate the fruit of their own free will. It was a choice they each made.

KNOWLEDGE IS POWER

It is power that tempted Eve—she wanted the power of knowing the difference between good and evil, she wanted to be like God. But once she and Adam had knowledge of good and evil, they were cast out of the Garden into our world, where humans have free will and need to confront good and evil every day, a world where we are responsible for the choices we make and their consequences.

Whether from genocide or carbon emissions or something we've said or done that seems minor, everything we do and say has consequences. *Everything.*

RAISING CAIN

The phrase "raising Cain" has at least two interpretations. One is the raising of children—and Adam and Eve did not do such a great job if Cain is any indication.

A parent's mission is to bring a child up in the world, to literally raise an infant to the level where s/he can function independently, to lift them to a higher spiritual ground. It is the parents' job to prepare their child to be an adult who can think critically and has moral values, to teach them to be responsible and accountable for their own actions.

The second interpretation of "raising Cain" is to cause a commotion. Sometimes that's a good thing and sometimes not so much. One can cause a commotion for selfish reasons, or one can choose to do so for altruistic reasons—because one cares about others.

Cain was Adam and Eve's oldest son. He worked hard and tilled the fields, earning his food by the sweat of his brow. Their second son, Abel, was a shepherd. His sacrifices to God were more acceptable than Cain's, and Cain resented it. Cain's emotions were clearly evident. When God asked Cain, "Why are you upset?" He essentially warns him that giving in to dejection and rage and losing his temper will cause him to go down the path of self-destruction and do things he will regret.

Cain disregards the advice, loses his temper and kills his brother. When questioned, he tries to blame God by saying He should have stopped him. That doesn't work; Cain is held accountable and is punished.

When asked, "Where is your brother?" Cain retorted, "Am I my brother's keeper?" The unspoken answer is, "You'd better believe it!"

Anyone who has ever felt that a parent favored a sibling over him or her understands why Cain was angry. Sibling rivalry is an old story, and Cain was just the first in a long line of people throughout history, including kings, princes and queens, who kill their siblings. Killing a family member is a terrible crime; killing *any* innocent person is a terrible crime.

We tend to forget that all human beings are members of the same family; we all share common DNA — the genetic code that links us all together. (The National Geographic Human Genome Project is conducting research to determine exactly how we are all connected.[4])

As such, we are, under the skin, all brothers and sisters, and we are, indeed, responsible for one another.

Imagine if aliens from another galaxy come to attack this planet. Do we think they would notice our differences? To them all humans are humans, whether they are black, white, yellow, red, Jewish, Christian, Muslim, Hindu, gay, atheist, communist, democrat, republican, whatever…to them it would make no difference at all.

TO SERVE MAN

The *Twilight Zone*, a popular science fiction TV series in the 1960s, aired an episode that clearly made the above point. Aliens come to Earth and say they will bring peace and prosperity to everyone on the planet. To prove their point they present scientists with a book entitled *To Serve Man.**

Mankind soon enjoys the benefits of the aliens' presence. They even visit the aliens' world and send back postcards

*Watch a short clip about this at:
http://www.youtube.com/watch?v=WudBfRa0ETw
There is also a full episode at:
http://www.cbs.com/classics/the_twilight_zone/video/video.php?cid=649562032&pid=W4F0L_skkbpXGUnd7Qu3nO1bLGyk0Ihm&play=true&cc=2

about how wonderful things are. It is only when the book is translated that humans discover it is a cookbook and that Planet Earth is the cattle ranch. Guess who was on the menu? Everyone. No one is spared.

In 1969, *Star Trek*, another popular science-fiction series, aired an episode called, "Let That Be Your Last Battlefield." There were two groups of people living on a planet. Both had faces that were black on one side and white on the other. But some had black on the left and white on the right and some had black on the right and white on the left. For that minor difference they destroyed their peoples and the entire planet. Even when only two of them were left, one from each "side," the battle continued to the death. Brothers under the skin, they nevertheless committed genocide on each other.*

KILLING THE FUTURE

When God asked Cain, "What have you done? Your brother's blood is crying out from the ground," in the original Biblical text, the Hebrew word for blood in this verse is in the plural. According to Jewish scholars, Cain is responsible not just for the death of Abel, but also for his unborn descendants, because the potential of each of those individuals would never be realized.

Imagine how many potentialities disappear when millions of innocent people are murdered.

BLAMING COMES NATURALLY

The natural response when we are "caught" doing something wrong or stupid is to blame someone else; we absolve ourselves so that we do not live with regret, shame and guilt.

When things don't turn out well, or don't go as planned, no one wants to take responsibility or be held accountable for

*See http://www.imdb.com/video/cbs/vi2437218329

his or her actions or inactions. On the other hand, everyone wants credit when something turns out great, whether or not s/he was responsible. That's human nature.

That's why almost every family in the world has an invisible child whose name is NOT ME. How do we know this? Often, in every family, when someone asks "Who spilled the milk? or "Who left the lights on?" or "Who kept the door open?" and "Who didn't flush the toilet?" someone answers, "NOT ME."

TEMPTATION

Temptation, the evil inclination that exists in all of us, is symbolized by many as "the snake." Yet temptation is the *human* challenge. The snake as a symbol of evil is known from the most primitive tribal cultures to the most intellectually sophisticated societies.

Even in our modern culture, the snake continues to be used as a symbol of evil. For instance, J.K. Rowling, in her *Harry Potter* series, uses the snake as the defining symbol of evil: Voldemort and the Slytherin.

Hitler said, "Kill the Jews," and the Germans and their collaborators did as he asked. Their snake was Nazism and its quest for political power, economic stability at any cost, and racial domination of the world. To achieve those goals, the Germans and their collaborators made the decision to kill millions upon millions of men, women, and children of all ages.

The snake embodies the dangers and consequences of free will. We can choose to do selfish, ego-boosting, and immoral acts. That gives us a sense of power and entitlement. It can also serve us as a reminder to do the opposite: acts of compassion, decency, justice, and honor.

CHAPTER THREE

CHOICES, CHOICES, CHOICES

I would also like to say that it did not at all occur to me that these orders could be unjust. It is true that I know that it is also the duty of the police to protect the innocent, but I was then of the conviction that the Jews were not innocent but guilty. I believed the propaganda that all Jews were criminals and sub-humans and that they were the cause of Germany's decline after the First World War. The thought that one should disobey or evade the orders to participate in the extermination of the Jews did not therefore enter my mind at all.

Kurt Mobius
Former Police Battalion Member
who served in the Chelmno massacres,
testifying in Poland on November 8, 1961[1]

IN COLD BLOOD

As part of the plan to rid the German Fatherland and its occupied territories of their Jewish inhabitants, *Einsatzgruppen*, special Nazi killing and looting squads, were created. One of these, Reserve Police Battalion 101, began its tour of duty in the Lublin Region of Poland in 1942. The group consisted of truck drivers, dock workers, clerks and salesmen who had never seen combat—average German citizens plus some men from Luxembourg. They were assigned to round up Jews and herd them into ghettos and camps. As they followed German troops eastward, in one small town after another, they were also ordered to shoot the Jews *en masse*.[2]

For Battalion 101's first assignment (on July 13, 1942), commanding officer Major Wilhelm Trapp ordered the troops to remove 300 able-bodied Jewish males from the town of Jozefow for slave labor. They were then ordered to shoot the 1,500 Jewish women, children, and elderly left behind. If any of the men "did not feel up to the task," he said, they did not have to participate in the killing. *Only a dozen men opted out.*

It took 16 hours for the rest of the battalion to fulfill its assignment. Each and every person was shot by a member of Battalion 101 who aimed his pistol or rifle directly at his victim and pulled the trigger. At the end of the day, Trapp's men were covered in blood and gore.[3]

By the time they were mustered out, these otherwise "normal" people had slaughtered the Jews of Jozefow,

Lomazy, Miedzyrzec, Serokomla, Kotsk, and Lukow. All
told, they were responsible for the shooting deaths of more
than 38,000 Jews and the deportation of almost 45,000
others to Treblinka, the Nazi extermination camp. What's
more, they bragged about what they had done and took
"trophy" photos, smiling and laughing in the presence of
their victims.[4]

Nazi war crimes documents have records of 333,082
individuals in 4,105 units and agencies who were involved, or
suspected of being involved in this killing. Many of the lists
are incomplete, and there still are many institutions that have
not been investigated. Daniel Goldhagen, in *Hitler's Willing
Executioners*, says he would not be surprised if the number
of people involved in direct killing exceeded 500,000.[5]

THE NUREMBERG WAR CRIMES TRIALS

At the end of World War II, the Allies set about putting
Nazi war criminals on trial. Among the charges were
"crimes against the peace" and "crimes against humanity."
Specific crimes against the Jews were not raised. These crimes
were subsumed in the general category of Crimes Against
Humanity. Later, specific trials were held that made specific
references to the "The Final Solution." [See "Concise History
of the Holocaust."] The first trial of 45 SS men and women
and some kapos (prisoner functionaries) from the Auschwitz
and Bergen-Belsen camps, was a British military tribunal at
Lüneburg, Germany, held in September-November, 1945.
There, for the first time, former prisoners testified publicly
about the torture and mass murder. In November, 21 top
Nazis were tried before the International Military Tribunal
at Nuremberg, Germany. They included Hermann Goering,
Hitler's designated successor and head of the SA (the
private army of the Nazi Party), Joachim von Ribbentropp,
Hitler's foreign minister, and Albert Speer, Hitler's favorite
architect, who became his Minister of Armaments and War
Production.

"These trials established the proposition that men and

women who commit war crimes can be brought to justice and made to pay for their crimes, not by summary execution but in a court of law," explains Menachem Z. Rosensaft, Adjunct Professor of Law at Cornell Law School, where his specialty is war crimes trials.

"Perhaps, most importantly, while the defendants at Nuremberg were charged with war crimes, they were also charged with crimes against humanity. This made clear to the world that civilized society cannot condone acts of genocide and will hold those responsible legally accountable," says Rosensaft.

ABSOLUTELY SHOCKING!

In April 1961, Adolf Eichmann, the man who initiated and facilitated industrialized murder and organized the transportation for the deportations of European Jewry, went on trial in Jerusalem. When he was put on trial, he used the "I was following orders" defense. But Eichmann was not a cog in the machine who was just "following orders." He and his cohorts developed and issued the orders for the extermination of the Jews.

Captured in Argentina in May 1960 by Mossad, the Israeli intelligence agency, Eichmann's trial was televised around the world. [He was ultimately convicted and hanged.]

That same summer, Stanley Milgram, a Yale University psychologist, asked: "Could it be that Eichmann and his million accomplices in the Holocaust *were* just following orders?" He devised a controversial experiment designed to answer that question.[6]

Milgram's experiment focused on the relationship between punishment and learning. He established a scenario that a "student," who could not be seen but could be heard, was strapped to a chair in another area and connected to "electrical

*http://www.archive.org/details/1961-04-13_Eichmann_trial

wires" that would ostensibly deliver a series of shocks from 15 to 450 volts. The "teachers" were told that the "students" would not suffer permanent damage, but that it would be very painful for them if they did not respond correctly.

In the experiment the "teacher" is convinced that he is harming another person for a higher cause, namely obeying "scientific authority." The "experimenter," who gave the "teacher" instructions, wore a white lab coat bespeaking that image of scientific authority. And so, as the experiment proceeded, if the "student" gave a wrong answer the "teacher" was ordered by the "experimenter" to give the student an electrical jolt.

As the "test" progressed, the "teachers" were ordered to give stronger and stronger shocks to the "students." The "teachers" could hear the students' screams and pounding in agony (all staged), but the "teachers" were supposed to continue until the 450-volt jolt was given.

The result of the experiment was that 65 percent of the everyday, normal people who participated as "teachers" in this experiment obeyed orders. They did so even when they knew they were causing someone great pain. But Milgram's experiment didn't require the "teachers" to be creative or take initiative. All they did was follow orders. Milgram concluded, "Obedience to authority, long praised as a virtue, takes on a new aspect when it serves a malevolent cause."

The Milgram experiment proved that most people will follow orders given by authority figures. When he was asked whether something like the Holocaust could occur in the United States, Milgram responded, "If a system of death camps were set up in the United States of the sort we had seen in Nazi Germany, one would be able to find sufficient personnel for those camps in any medium-sized American town."[7]

Is there equivalence between the acts of the men of Battalion 101 in their followng orders and Milgram's test subjects? The men of Battalion 101 were culled from the masses that had long been indoctrinated into believing that killing Jews was a proper thing to do—after all, their government, their church, and their history espoused it. Thus they had no problem facing their victims and dispatching them in any grisly manner they desired. Milgram's students, who could not see their "victims," were under the impression that what they were doing they did for a higher purpose, for a person they perceived to be a legitimate authority.

Are the situations the same? You decide.

WE GET TO CHOOSE

When Sacha Baron Cohen, a movie star who was once a member of the British Board of Jewish Deputies, made his smash hit film *Borat*, it stirred up a hornet's nest.[8] While Cohen's movie was "fiction," he filmed candid, unrehearsed responses to his outrageous behavior as he traveled through American towns and cities. One thing his movie showed is that as we cross America, the hatred for others unlike ourselves sits just beneath the surface. It only took a few minutes for groups of otherwise decent people to start singing, "In My Country Is a Problem/Throw the Jew Down the Well" with great gusto.[8*]

If you were sitting in that bar, what would you do? Would you stay to watch the show and sing along? Would you sit there fuming? Would you walk out without saying a word? Would you say something to the people in the bar before walking out? Would you ask to see the manager and demand your money back?

Watching the faces in the clip from *Borat*, we can see how quickly unthinking choices are made. We forget prejudice kills. We decide what we believe about others. We decide about the things we want to do or won't—whether to live in the moment, for instant gratification, or to think about

*This video clip can be seen on youtube.com. http://www.youtube.com/watch?v=Vb3IMTJjzfo

the long-term consequences of our actions and our moral
obligations.

What we decide determines the path our lives take and the
content of our character. It will define who we are as human
beings and as members of our community.

THE COMFORT ZONE

If we know ourselves well enough to know how to
ethically respond to a *Borat*-like situation, and consider
ourselves good people, we sometimes believe we are doing
more good than we actually do. There are comfortable
ways to convince ourselves that we are making a difference
when we are not. We brand ourselves as caring persons
by identifying publicly with a cause by wearing a T-shirt,
a ribbon or pin. But wearing something does not make
things change. Neither does watching a film. Neither does
putting a sign on the lawn that says "No more genocide."
It makes us feel good, but if we want to make a difference,
we need to take real action.

IT'S NOT EASY BEING GOOD

Dr. Philip Zimbardo, a psychologist at Stanford University,
conducted simulated prison experiments and concluded
that situations cause the way people behave. He found that
their moral viewpoints did not come into play.[9] [Zimbardo's
conclusion was that the situation caused the way people
behaved, and that their moral viewpoints did not come into
play. Others disagreed with him. Leading psychologists,
including Erich Fromm, objected to the way the experiment
was designed and declared it unethical. He also claimed the
results were flawed.]

Professor Zimbardo created a laboratory of 24 prisoners
and guards who were divided randomly and placed into
a situation in which each was to play their assigned role
for two weeks. They were selected from a group of college
students who answered a newspaper ad to volunteer in a

psychological study of "prison life," and were tested before so as to rule out anyone who showed any tendency towards rigid adherence to conventional values and a submissive, uncritical attitude toward authority.

The simulation began with wailing police sirens as nine young men were picked up at their homes, frisked, handcuffed, taken to a police station, fingerprinted and booked before being blindfolded and driven to a "prison" in the basement of the Stanford psychology building. There, three young men dressed as guards supervised their activities in a prison-like cell with cots, a small yard and a solitary confinement "hole."

All were instructed not to use physical punishment or aggression but to simulate dehumanizing conditions of prison life. They were to spray prisoners with a "delousing" liquid, fit them with a chain and lock around one ankle, dress prisoners in loosely-fitted smocks with no underclothes. Guards were given uniforms, whistles, and nightsticks for their eight-hour shifts. Videotapes and audio recordings quickly showed that the guard's involvement went far beyond the role-playing. They started to enjoy their power by refusing to let the prisoners go to the toilet, insulting and humiliating them. By the end of the sixth day the study had to be terminated because the prisoners were getting extremely depressed, anxious and angry, and the guards were out of control.

As Dr. Eva Fogelman indicates, "When people are put into certain situations and roles, they behave in ways that they ordinarily would not behave. The Freudian idea is that when people are in a group it gives them permission to behave in more extreme ways—a sort of herd mentality takes over."[10] Years later, in 2004, when it was revealed American troops were torturing prisoners in Iraq. Zimbardo, who understood the mentality of the prison guards because of his experiment, compared the soldiers at Abu Ghraib (an American prison in Iraq) to the members of Battalion 101. He said, "Like the photos of the guards of Abu Ghraib Prison, these [Nazi] policemen put themselves in their trophy photos as proud killers of the Jewish menace."[11]

We all have choices. We do not have to glory in evil as did the members of Battalion 101. The snake does not make us do anything we do not want to do.

REPAIRING THE WORLD

In the Jewish tradition there is an obligation called *Tikkun Olam*, to repair the world. The goal is to make the world a better place for everyone by doing good deeds—from helping the poor, funding education, to making beneficial scientific discoveries. The tradition also understands that repairing the world is an overwhelming responsibility. Jewish scholars in the first century C.E. said: "It is not your responsibility to finish the work [of perfecting the world], but you are not free to desist from it either.[12]

*N*othing is so contagious as example; and we never do any great good or evil which does not produce its like.

Francois de La Rochefoucauld

*F*reedom is not merely the opportunity to do as one pleases; neither is it merely the opportunity to choose between set alternatives. Freedom is, first of all, the chance to formulate the available choices, to argue over them — and then, the opportunity to choose.

C. Wright Mills

CHAPTER FOUR

FREEDOM IS A PRIVILEGE

*A*s unimaginable as it seems, slavery and bondage still persist in the early 21st century. Millions of people around the world still suffer in silence in slave-like situations of forced labor and commercial sexual exploitation from which they cannot free themselves. Trafficking in persons is one of the greatest human rights challenges of our time.

U.S. State Department
"Trafficking in Persons Report," June 2003[1]

In America, we enjoy the privilege of freedom. We think it is our right, but it is a right we earn by being participants in the governing process. It works like this: If we don't vote, we really don't have the right to complain. If we dismiss the process and stop paying attention to what our leaders are doing, we may wake up one morning to discover, like the Germans did, that we no longer have a real voice. If we want the continued privilege of freedom, we need to pay attention to what is happening in the world around us and respond to it in constructive and helpful ways and make sure we are heard when we see governments perpetrating injustice. Once injustice rears its head, anything can happen, including genocide.

CAN GENOCIDE HAPPEN IN AMERICA?

Genocide can happen anywhere the rule of law collapses, when governments are misguided or politicians are corrupted. Even in America.

How do we know that?

While not committing genocide *per se,* we do know America committed genocidal acts against Native Americans. Native Americans were labeled as uncouth savages. Whenever a treaty was made between Native Americans and the colonists, and eventually with the American government, it was invariably broken. This became so systematic that in 1830 the Indian Removal Act was passed, formally pushing all Native Americans out of their ancestral lands.

Under U.S. President Andrew Jackson, native lands were confiscated and death marches, like the Cherokee Trail of Tears in 1838-39, were organized to transfer natives from their ancestral territories to different, less hospitable regions in the West.* Native Americans were also forced to convert to Christianity with children being forcibly separated from their parents, given Christian names and put into boarding schools with the idea that educating them to "American" norms would destroy their Native American culture.[2]

Mary Hill of the Muskogee Tribe from Okfuskee Town (tulwa), Okemah, Oklahoma, told the story of her grandmother, Sallie Farney, who was among those forced to make the trip West from Alabama. (The stories from the Trail of Tears sound very familiar to those of Holocaust survivors who experienced their own death marches.**)

"The command for a removal came unexpectedly upon most of us. There was the time that we noticed that several overloaded wagons were passing our home, yet we did not grasp the meaning…Wagons stopped at our home and the men in charge commanded us to gather what few belongings could be crowded into the wagons. We were to be taken away and leave our homes, never to return. This was just the beginning of much weeping and heartaches…Many fell by the wayside, too faint with hunger or too weak to keep up with the rest. The aged, feeble, and sick were left to perish by the wayside…"[3]

---

*Oral histories of those who were forced from their homelands in the south and other areas are available at the Sequoya Research Center at the University of Arkansas, Little Rock.
http://www.anpa.ualr.edu/digital_library/indianvoices/family_stories/Hill.htm
** http://www.nowpublic.com/nazi_death_marches_horror_story_released

HATE SPEECH AND PROPAGANDA IN THE U.S.

In the 1920s, Henry Ford Sr., founder of the Ford Motor Company, reprinted *The Protocols of the Elders of Zion* – the Czarist Russian hoax that posits that Jews are engaged in an international conspiracy to control the world – in the newspaper the *Dearborn Independent*. As a result of a lawsuit, he was forced to recant. Though the lawsuit ended in a mistrial and Ford never testified, he issued public statements and apologies to individuals and Jews as a group. But it was hard to put the genie back in the bottle. The lie spread like wildfire.

Ku Klux Klan editors later assembled 96 of Henry Ford's antisemitic essays from the *Independent* and bound them in a volume called *The International Jew*, which was reprinted in Germany by the Nazi World Service.

On January 12, 1942, an embarrassed Henry Ford II (Henry Sr.'s son) wrote to the Klan's Imperial Wizard to say that he did "not subscribe to or support, directly or indirectly, any agitation which would promote antagonism against my Jewish fellow citizens," and threatened legal action.[4]

(After the Holocaust, Henry Ford II helped the Israelis build their first truck factories.)

At the Nuremberg War Crimes Trials after the war, two of the 21 defendants – Hitler Youth leader Baldur von Schirach and Radio Propaganda Chief Hans Fritzsche – cited the German edition of *The International Jew* as a major influence on their antisemitic views.

And it still hasn't ended. On June 10, 2009, the violent hate speech of white supremacists led to the murder of Stephen Tyrone Johns, a special security officer at the United States Holocaust Memorial Museum in Washington, D.C. It was later discovered that the killer maintained his own website to express rabid hatred of Jews and Blacks.

INTERNMENT CAMPS IN AMERICA

During World War II, President Franklin D. Roosevelt issued Executive Order 9066 to remove 120,000 Japanese and Japanese-Americans (more than 60 percent of them U.S. citizens) from their homes on the West Coast. He said this was done for the sake of "homeland security" because there was concern about a "fifth column" that, in addition to spying and committing sabotage, could signal enemy aircraft or ships coming from Japan in the Pacific.

To accomplish this task, Japanese-Americans from all of California and most of Oregon and Washington State were forcibly moved to military-created "exclusion zones." Most were sent to "War Relocation Centers" in isolated areas of Arizona, Arkansas, California, Colorado, Idaho, Utah, and Wyoming. In tar paper shacks and barbed-wire compounds guarded by armed guards, Japanese-American citizens were subjected to American concentration camp life. In 1944, the Supreme Court upheld the constitutionality of those camps and the separation of people of Japanese, Italian and German origins from American society. The court argued that it was permissible to curtail the civil rights of a group when there was a "pressing public necessity."

Eventually, some compensation for property losses was paid to Japanese-Americans in 1948, but there were no apologies until 1988, when President Ronald Reagan signed legislation that stated that "race prejudice, war hysteria, and a failure of political leadership" were behind the executive order. In 1990, the U.S. government began paying reparations to the Japanese families who were interned.[5]

NAZIS, SLAVERY & HUMAN TRAFFICKING

One of the principle crimes committed by the Nazis during World War II was the enslavement of millions of people throughout Europe. The slogan emblazoned above the gates of Auschwitz and other concentration and labor camps read

"Work Makes [You] Free." The sign was but a callous attempt at irony: Freedom only came after being worked to death.

Slavery is nothing new. Astonishingly, most slavery in the Western World was not officially abolished until less than 200 years ago. It was a way of life in every culture of the Old and New Worlds. And it is still acceptable in Southern Sudan, Niger, South Asia, and India, where international laws against slavery are not enforced. In India and Africa people are still born into castes of bonded servitude; child slavery is rampant.

It took a bloody civil war to end slavery in America, where for almost three centuries most black people lived as slaves. In 1619, African slaves were brought to Jamestown, the British colony in Virginia. After the establishment of the United States in 1776, slaves and freemen were victims of government-sanctioned violence regulated by Black Codes. These were enforced by white people who used summary punishment, including maiming, lynching, and other forms of murder against escaped slaves.

(On July 30, 2008, the U.S. House of Representatives issued a formal apology to Black Americans for the institution of slavery in America. The resolution was initiated by Representative Steven Cohen, a white Jew representing a Black district in Memphis. A year later, on June 19, 2009, the U.S. Senate issued a similar apology.)

SLAVERY TODAY

Though slavery has generally been outlawed, as long as money is to be made from the sale of human beings, slavery will continue. Recently, the United States Department of State discovered that some international peacekeepers in areas of conflict engage in human trafficking. Sex slave trafficking, which includes children, exists in Africa, Thailand, China, the Middle East, including Israel, Central Europe, and the Balkans, Eastern European countries, and the Americas, including the

United States. It is a huge business that makes billions of dollars annually and costs thousands of innocent lives.

LONG PROSS, 21ST CENTURY SLAVE CHILD

New York Times columnist Nicholas Kristof marked the beginning of 2009 with a plea against the trafficking of girls into brothels. In his column on January 4, he wrote about a teenage girl, Long Pross, a child who looks, he says, "like a normal, fun-loving girl, with a pretty face and a joyous smile. Then move around, and you see where her brothel owner gouged out her right eye."

He knows it's hard for his readers to see his words on paper, but describes how much harder it is for Pross to tell the story of what happened to her and allow herself to be taped. But she gathered her strength to do it, "because she wants people to understand how brutal sex trafficking can be."

A woman kidnapped Pross in Cambodia when she was 13 and sold her into a brothel run by another woman. She was tortured until she agreed to cooperate, locked up and bound, except when she was working. As a virgin she was sold for a premium price—four times over. She was beaten and tortured with electrical shocks daily. Some of the other girls were murdered. Twice she was forced to have painful abortions. When she asked for some respite after the second one, her owner gouged her eye out with a piece of metal.

Kristof writes that when Pross' eye became infected, her owner discarded her. She was rescued by Somaly Mam, a trafficking survivor who started a foundation in Cambodia to fight sexual slavery. Kristof also wrote that this "business model of forced prostitution is remarkably similar from Pakistan to Vietnam—and, sometimes, in the United States as well. Pimps and gangs, organized crime and others, use

---

* You can see a video about Pross at http://video.nytimes.com/video/2009/01/03/opinion/1194837193498/the-face-of-slavery.html

violence, humiliation, and narcotics to shatter girls' self-esteem and terrorize them into unquestioning, instantaneous obedience."[6]

His blog at *www.nytimes.com/on the ground* is where you can find more detailed information about human trafficking and the terrible toll it takes on young people.*

HOW TO EMPOWER YOURSELF TO EFFECT CHANGE

People in power—the decision makers, the politicians and media moguls, the CEO's of institutions and corporations—may seem indifferent to anything but their own power. In reality, these movers and shakers are extremely sensitive to public opinion. They care about getting reelected. They care about ratings and sales. People really care about staying in power and will do whatever they need to do to stay there, even if it means that they have to listen to the public.

We are the public. By working together, we can create a powerful force. We can use that power to control what our political and corporate leaders do. We vote. We buy the products. We watch the programs, and we get to decide who gets our money and attention.

But to be effective, people need correct information. Confirm the information you receive with more than one or two sources. If you think something doesn't ring true, there's a good chance you are right, especially if it doesn't make sense.

Go to the source.

WHAT ABOUT AMERICA?

In America no one yet knows who the next target of discrimination and hatred might be. But if a target population is chosen as "the other," like the Japanese-

Americans, German-Americans and Italian-Americans
were during World War II, we must remember that we
are human beings with human weaknesses. We share the
same DNA, we are all made the same way, and we are our
brothers' and sisters' keepers.

History is never proved, only supposed. No matter how much evidence you collect, you're always guessing about cause-and-effect, and assuming things about dead people's motives. Since even living people don't understand their own motives, we're hardly likely to do any better with the dead.

Keep testing your guesses against the evidence. Keep trying out new guesses to see if they fit better. Keep looking for new evidence, even if it disproves your old hypotheses. With each step you get just a little closer to that elusive things called "the truth." With each step you see how much farther away the truth is than you ever imagined it to be.[7]

Orson Scott Card
Empire

*C*hange will not come if we wait for some other person or some other time. We are the ones we've been waiting for. We are the change that we seek.

Barack Obama
44th U.S. President*

*http://www.barackobama.com/2008/02/05/remarks_of_sena-
tor_barack_obam_46.php

CHAPTER FIVE

JIMINY CRICKET

Universal ethical values are expressed in what are commonly known as the Ten Commandments or the Ten Pronouncements, the basic moral/ethical values. They are the basis of the rule of law at the heart of the Abrahamic faiths—particularly the Judeo-Christian ethics of Western civilization. They are the basis for the American system of law. We might compare these rules to western civilization's conscience, the Jiminy Cricket of society. Just as Jiminy Cricket warned Pinocchio to do the right thing, these ethical values drive the conscience of the moral world.

Adolf Hitler intended to undermine the Judeo-Christian ethic that had been accepted in Europe for millennia. He understood that those ethics would stand in the way of his grand plan to create a master race and a Thousand-Year Reich. But he was unwilling to attack the churches directly and instead attacked their origins—Judaism and the Jewish people. He strove to create a society that would operate on impulse and animal instinct, with no distinction between right and wrong.

Robert Wistrich in *Antisemitism – the Longest Hatred*, wrote: "Nazism itself became contaminated with a profound Christophobia, decrying Christianity as a 'Semitic' religion which was emasculating the healthy, heroic and warrior virtues of the German people with its preaching of the virtues of humility, compassion, charity and love."[1]

ETHICS AND VALUES ARE NOT THE SAME

According to ethicist Michael Josephson, "Ethics refers to principles that define behavior as right, good and proper. [*ed. note:* Just because the Nazis said that what they were doing was right, good and proper, did not make it so.] Such principles do not always dictate a single 'moral' course of action, but provide a means of evaluating and deciding among competing options. ...The terms 'ethics' and 'values' are not interchangeable. Ethics is concerned with how a moral person should behave, whereas values are the inner judgments that determine how a person actually behaves. Values concern ethics when they pertain to beliefs about what is right and wrong. Most values, however, have nothing to do with ethics...."[2] (*See Appendix Two* – Six Pillars of Character)

PEOPLE BUILT AUSCHWITZ

This book is not meant to be a treatise or speculation on God, good or evil. We are not writing theology. We are trying to be practical and describe what is observable about people's behavior. For some, the Holocaust is all about God. For purposes of our discussion in this book, it's about people and the way they behave.

The Nazis and their collaborators were people who had an ideology that demanded the death of every single Jew and the destruction of Judeao-Christian religion. Those people built the gas chambers, made the trains run and turned in their neighbors. Blaming God for their actions does not work because it absolves the perpetrator from responsibility — and whether we believe in God or not, we are all still responsible for our actions.

At the Bronx Zoo in New York City, there was a sign hanging on a wall in the Ape House. The words read: THE MOST DANGEROUS CREATURE ON EARTH. The sign was not printed on paper. It was printed on a mirror.

People shot men, women, and children and threw them into pits. People herded millions into cattle cars to be used as slaves or murdered. In every war in history, especially during World War II and the Holocaust, human beings inflicted the worst possible harm on other human beings. The Nazis and their collaborators chose to kill their own babies first and then killed millions upon millions of children, adults and the elderly. Stalin, Pol Pot and Mao tortured and murdered millions. The Janjaweed in Darfur are agents of the Sudanese government. The Chinese sent troops to Tibet. People have done evil things to other people since Cain killed Abel.

In the Holocaust, most people were bystanders who did nothing to stop the evil around them, just like the people who watched Kitty Genovese die. Some became thieves. Some became killers. A few — too few — became rescuers. That was their choice.

Natural disasters are the natural consequences of the laws of Nature. A lion killing a gazelle is not an evil act — it is a lion being a lion. A tsunami is the result of an underwater earthquake. And an earthquake is a natural act — the planet behaving like a planet.

San Francisco is hit by an earthquake and people are killed. So why is the city constantly rebuilt on an active crack in the ground that everyone knows is going to cause more earthquakes and death in the future? Why do people build skyscrapers in hurricane zones? It's because people don't think about the long term consequences of their actions. They think about the here and now. That's human nature. We forget about the dead and the destruction. Like Hitler said, "It's yesterday's news."

We do not live in a perfect world. We don't often see how the "bad guys" get punished. Sometimes good things happen to bad people and bad things happen to good people. That's life.

The true test of our humanity is how we respond to the victims of these natural disasters and acts of evil.

DESTROYING A WORLD

Even when the law of the land says we can kill and steal from our "enemies," that does not make it right. Self-respect and dignity come from doing the right thing, even if it is difficult. Bringing God into the equation and blaming God for things people do to one another is just another way of avoiding responsibility.

For the most part, the Jews were rounded up by average citizens ordered to do so by leaders who were driven by hate-fueled racism — zealous ideologues who figured out how to industrialize and commercialize a people's destruction. Men put their fellow men on trains driven by individuals; the camps and ghettos were guarded by individuals. Jews were tortured and shot by individuals. Individuals made the decisions of life and death for their fellow man.

Every horrible act in the Holocaust and other genocides was committed by individuals who made choices. They could have done what they had the right to do — to kill Jews (as legalized by their government). Or they could have done the right thing and resisted the pressures in their society and saved Jews, even when their own lives were at stake.

KOSOVO

The war between the Serbs (non-Muslims) and the Kosovars (Muslims) was nothing if not a morality tale for the post-Holocaust world. It began when Kosovo declared independence in February 1998. Slobodan Milosevic, the president of Serbia, and his paramilitary thugs, the Orthodox Christian Scorpions, initiated the techniques used by Hitler's *Einsatsgruppen*. Their victims were Muslim ethnic Albanians, the most moderate Muslims in the world. But this war was not a religious war, it was classic ethnic cleansing. And it began with rhetoric. Milosovic went on the air, used the newspapers, and made speeches accusing the "Albanians" of hogging the educational system, making demands and taking away jobs. Soon the Scorpions were running through Serbia and Kosovo selecting, looting, burning, raping, and killing as they cleansed out the "ethnics."

In 2001, in The Hague, the World Court indicted Milosevic, charging him with crimes against humanity and genocide for his role in all of the Balkan wars—Croatia, Bosnia and Kosovo. Milosevic died of a heart attack during the trial in 2006 and was never convicted.

At a war crimes trial in Belgrade, eight years later, a witness, a former Scorpion who feared for his life and was known only as P1, testified behind a curtain.

"I saw the civilians coming out of a house. First came an elderly man, then two women with children in their arms, followed by a girl and a boy. Then, hell broke loose," he said, with paramilitaries shooting and shouting: "Up against the wall, let's kill them all!"

The witness told the court he saw an ethnic Albanian woman crying after apparently being raped by a Scorpion. He described how the man then grabbed the woman by her hair, smashed her head against a wall and fired two shots at her. Though he could not identify the rapist, his ex-comrades were sentenced to 20 years in prison.[3]

When governments are complicit, neighbors find it easy to kill their neighbors for their cars, their computers, their jobs, and their money, all in the name of nationalism, religion or race.

CHAPTER SIX

THE LURE OF THE DARK SIDE

Of course I am a doctor and I want to preserve life. And out of respect for human life, I would remove a gangrenous appendix from a diseased body. The Jew is the gangrenous appendix in the body of mankind.[1]

SS Dr. Fritz Klein
a doctor at Auschwitz Concentration Camp

Have you ever asked yourself who educated Mengele, Freisler and the hundreds of well-trained doctors and lawyers who made the Nazi machine work? ...They weren't educated in Nazi universities. They were taught in world-renowned universities in a time when having a degree from a German university was as good as you could get.

Dr. Franklin H. Littell
Methodist minister, Holocaust scholar

Power tends to corrupt; and absolute power corrupts absolutely.

John Emerich Edward Dalberg-Acton

Maimonides, the medieval Jewish philosopher and physician, taught that free will means that our moral and spiritual characters are never set in stone. At every moment we are able to renew ourselves and achieve great spiritual heights by doing the right thing and taking responsibility. At the same time, we are at every moment tempted by the snake and can destroy a lifetime of good deeds by making even one bad choice.

There are individuals who choose to go over to the Dark Side, a.k.a. Evil. Like Darth Vader in *Star Wars*, they can be vengeful, angry and bitter, and work for people who use them for their own nefarious purposes. (In the end, Darth Vader sees the error of his ways and redeems himself by destroying the Empire that empowered him.)

Power is the central attraction of the Dark Side. People enjoy the power of controlling other people, and many times power that can be used for "good" is used instead to commit unethical and immoral acts. Most people who are evil feel that they are above the law, that they are exempt from mainstream societal mores and morals. Their sense of entitlement gives them a sense of superiority. (*See Appendix Three - Definition of a Sociopath.*)

IS EVIL BANAL?

Hannah Arendt, a philosopher who fled the Nazis, decided during the Adolf Eichmann trial in Jerusalem, that evil was banal — ordinary and humdrum — because she thought Eichmann was banal.

She was wrong. Evil is never banal, the evildoer may sometimes be banal, if he is the one who is simply following orders. But Eichmann was not following orders. He was evil and led evil men who believed that every Jew on the planet needed to be destroyed.

Based on documents that are now available, historians agree that there was nothing banal about Eichmann and the bureaucracy of which he was a part. In *Hitler's Bureaucrats: The Nazi Security Police and the Banality of Evil*, author Yaacov Lozowick clearly shows that Eichmann and his team were a group of people who were completely aware of what they were doing. They were people with high ideological motivation, who took the initiative and contributed far beyond what was necessary to achieve their murderous goals.

As he noted, "...there could be no doubt about it: they clearly understood that their deeds were not positive except in the value system of the Third Reich. They hated Jews and thought that getting rid of them would be to Germany's good."[2]

Hans Safrian, another historian (who wrote *Eichmann's Maenner*) described how Eichmann was the man who sent his forces across the continent to do their work there. He documented the conscious dedication that enveloped not only Eichmamn but his men as well. They were anything but banal. They followed and executed their racist ideology by taking the initiative, using innovation, zeal, and dedication. They may have been paper pushers for the most part, but when they made decisions they were ruthless in condemning people to their deaths.

Historian Yehuda Bauer has said, "Eichmann managed to fool her (Hannah Arendt), and many others. He was no cog. He was part of the machine motor. He was an initiator, and a convinced and extreme Nazi ideologist and antisemite. The bureaucratic group he was part of the *Reichssicherheitshauptamt* (RSHA), was ideologically motivated and was the moving spirit of the Nazi terror machine. The RSHA was responsible only to Himmler and

Hitler, and received their full support. It was the center of the terror regime. It was responsible for the *Einsatzgruppen*, for the Gestapo, for population movements, for the mass murders.

In many cases the evil doer is a sociopath obsessed with the uses of power. But evil acts are not confined to sociopaths. All of us — under the wrong circumstances — have the capacity to do evil if we make the wrong choices.

POWER TOOLS

Power can be defined in many ways. It is the ability to get what you want because you have the talent, method or tools to do so, whether by right or might.

The University of Colorado Conflict Research Consortium makes distinctions between three kinds of power — "power over," "power to" and "power with."[3]

"POWER OVER" means you control other people. Those in control can attempt to influence the masses with verbal persuasion. But if that doesn't work, if people don't want to do what they are told to do, the "controllers" can resort to using the violent tools of power: force, torture or threats. In most cases, when someone abuses his/her power, his/her victims become excessively dependent, and every aspect of their lives is controlled.

In a family dynamic this often manifests itself in domestic violence. In an organization or society, some leaders, usually the most charismatic, are given total power over their followers, who become their "subjects" and do as they are told. In addition to destroying their individuality, this absolves their followers from making choices and taking responsibility for their actions.

"POWER TO" means you have the ability, resources, and method to do whatever you want; it allows you to do things other people cannot or will not do.

"Power with" means that you bring together other entities
or people who will help you accomplish your goals. In
a positive world, it would be the equivalent of joining a
neighborhood watch group, or founding a committee to
build a park, or creating cooperation between groups or
individuals to get something accomplished for the benefit
of the community.

These same kinds of coalitions can be used to perpetrate evil.
In communist and fascist countries, people spy on and report
their neighbors for real and imagined acts. In these cases, as
in Nazi Germany, children are taught to inform on their own
parents and siblings. Family members who resist the party line
can land in jail or worse.

DOCTORS PLAYING AT GOD

A positive example of "power with" is Dr. Jonas Salk,
who used his power to stop a dread disease, polio, from
killing millions of children. Developing the polio vaccine, he
used the power of persuasion to convince medical experts and
government leaders that his discovery could save millions of
lives. He used his power "with" the power of others to make
the vaccine available worldwide.

Edward R. Murrow, then the dean of CBS reporters, wanted
to know if Salk had done it for the money. In 1955, in a
televised interview, he asked Salk who owned the patent
for the vaccine. Salk was surprised by the question. He said,
"Well, the people, I guess. There is no patent. Could you
patent the sun?"[4]

On the other hand, even before the establishment of the Third
Reich, German doctors were the staunchest supporters of the
Nazis. Starting in 1929, they were the first to kill "defective"
German babies on Hitler's orders. By 1942, 45 percent of non-
Jewish German doctors were members of the Nazi Party, a higher
percentage than any other group of German professionals. These
38,000 Nazi doctors viewed killing as a therapeutic imperative.
None of the German doctors who worked on human medical

experiments and were tried in Nuremberg ever admitted that what they did was wrong.

What could they have been thinking when they killed all those people?

The Hippocratic Oath, taken by doctors since ancient times, is a promise not to harm patients. During war crimes trials, 23 doctors who worked in Nazi concentration camps were found guilty of breaching the code of medical ethics by performing horrifying medical experiments on prisoners. This led to discussions regarding ethical treatment of human subjects and outlined the ethics of medical research with regard to the human rights of these subjects.[5]

In Auschwitz and other death and concentration camps, German doctors sold on Nazi ideology chose who would live long enough to be worked to death and who would be gassed, shot or hanged immediately. They also performed medical experiments on human beings without their consent, rarely using anesthetics. Among them were experiments to determine how quickly a poison or disease can kill, how long it takes a human being to freeze, and why twins do or don't have the same traits.

America has also not been innocent of such mad science. In the 1930s, American doctors were guilty of conducting human medical experiments based on race. On July 25, 1972, Associated Press reporter Jean Heller revealed the top-secret Tuskegee Syphilis Study that allowed a focus group of black men to go untreated for their disease. She wrote: "For 40 years, the U.S. Public Health Service has conducted a study in which human guinea pigs, not given proper treatment, have died of syphilis and its side effects…"[6]

One of the results of such medical experiments and their condemnation at the Nuremberg War Crimes Trials was the notion of "informed consent." In the United States, doctors cannot perform a medical procedure unless they advise the patient of their course of treatment and the patient agrees in writing. A patient also has the right to stop a procedure or treatment.

Using humans for medical experiments raises ethical issues. We need to consider these ethical dilemmas when we carry out human medical experiments to save lives today. We have to ask ourselves if assisted suicide in cases of terminal illness is acceptable. We need to ask ourselves if abortion is acceptable, and under what circumstances. Should people participate in clinical trials or drug tests, when those tests might cause them harm? Furthermore, is it ethical to suppress negative information? For instance, how do we deal with corporations that refuse to link tobacco inhalation to lung cancer and other diseases or those who "fail" to recognize dioxin as contributing to diseases in Vietnam veterans exposed to Agent Orange? What do we do when the government fails to acknowledge troop exposure to airborne contaminants during the 1990 Gulf War and how this affected 25 percent of Gulf War veterans?[7] What do we say to a government that refuses to extend health care benefits to wounded veterans and their families? And what of those who were affected by the pollution in New York City caused by the events of 9/11?

Mankind has been given the knowledge and ability to perfect the world. All we have to do is make ethical choices — and that is not always an easy thing to do. Good and evil co-exist. If there is no sadness, how can we know happiness? If there is no disease, how can we appreciate good health? If there is no war, why would we work toward peace? And if we don't know the difference between good and evil, how could we make the world a better place? Our responsibility is to resist the lure of the dark side.

According to the positive ethical laws, personal hygiene, clean hands that do no harm, and harmless passions and language are not enough; the decent person must have working hands, *he must be his brother's keeper. He must do what he can to prevent others from violating the negative laws of a life-and-death ethic.*

Philip Hallie
Lest Innocent Blood Be Shed

T*he only thing necessary for the triumph of evil is for good men to do nothing.*

Edmund Burke
British statesman

W*hen evil men plot, good men must plan. When evil men burn and bomb, good men must build and bind. When evil men shout ugly words of hatred, good men must commit themselves to the glories of love.*

Martin Luther King, Jr.
Civil Rights leader

CHAPTER SEVEN

WORDS CAN KILL

༄

The 1948 convention on the Prevention and Punishment of the Crime of Genocide makes it as much of a crime to incite acts of genocide as to physically commit them. Incitement is generated by words—on paper, in music, on the radio, on TV and on the Internet. It's all about words and how they are used—and how we absorb and act on them.

Hate speech works because it appeals to the emotions, not to critical judgment. Most people hold opinions fostered by the societies they live in. These opinions, if not critically analyzed, can cause fear, hatred and violence toward others.

But the big lie used in genocide can also be used by a single person to destroy another person's life. Bullying is how power and hatred are manifested, especially among children.

Megan Meier, a 13-year-old who suffered from depression and attention deficit disorder, was harassed by a friend's mother, who posed as a teenage boy on myspace.com. Initially befriending Megan, after one month the poseur turned on her and emailed messages telling her that she was cruel, a fat slut, and that the world would be a better place without her. The next day, Megan hanged herself. Lori Drew, the woman who posted the messages, was convicted and sentenced to three years in prison.[1]

CREATING "THE OTHER"

The use of incitement with words, music, and images are "a critical causal element in genocide," according to Susan Benesch, a human rights expert:

> Incitement is a hallmark of genocide... and may be a prerequisite for it. Each modern case of genocide has been preceded by a propaganda campaign transmitted via mass media and directed by a handful of political leaders. If such campaigns could be stopped — or their masterminds deterred — genocide might be averted.

> Before genocide can occur, a large number of people must come to condone killing. The masses of people must be accustomed to treating this group to be attacked and persecuted as being separate from society.

> As the genocide scholar Helen Fein notes in describing this collective psychological process, one group of people must re-categorize another group of people as outside 'the boundaries of the universe of obligation.'[2]

If we dimish and dehumanize a group, then we can treat them inhumaely. It can begin with name calling and bullying and can end in murder. It doesn't have to, but it can. Once we consider our friends and neighbors vermin then we can deal with them as vermin. After all, if we call someone a cockroach long enough, we come to believe that we can step on them, just like we step on a bug. Pretty soon there are too many bugs and we call in the exterminator.

Wars, for example, are rife with this behavior. During the Korean War (1950-1953) opposing forces were labeled as "zipperheads" [when a bullet entered the enemy's head it opened like a zipper]. In Vietnam (1965-1975), U.S. military slang labeled Vietnamese as "gooks." Dehumanizing opponents makes them easier to kill.

Nowehere was this practice more formailzed than during the Nazi era. Julius Streicher, founder and editor of *Der*

Stürmer, the Nazi propaganda newspaper, worked with Nazi Propaganda Minister Joseph Goebbels to label Jews as vermin, sex offenders, thieves, liars, and killers. He described them as pests unworthy of existence and as conspiring, evil maniacs seeking control of the world. All of it was lies, but because of the unstable economic and political situation after World War I, the lies were readily believed.

Lies were also believed in Rwanda, in Bosnia, and in Kosovo. Hate speech prepared the average citizen to become an accomplice to murder.

ALL HATE, ALL THE TIME

Totalitarian governments take control of all forms of media as soon as they come into power. These non-democratic governments then dominate and manipulate their media for self-aggrandizing purposes. Truth becomes irrelevant.

This ability to use all media to promote a single point of view wears down and influences masses of people. Thus the media becomes a target whenever those seeking control of the populace come into power. Government control of the media took place in Venezuela and Russia in 2007. In addition to traditional media, China (as as do other countries) controls its nation's Internet access, because the Internet gives people nontraditional means to spread information. The American government controls the media, to a certain extent, via regulatory agencies that monitor them. When there is a war — whether conventional or not — many constitutional liberties, including free speech, can be curtailed, even in America.

Benesch describes how in the 1990s, when Serbian forces took over many television transmitters in Bosnia and Herzegovina, that large areas were dominated by Serbian propaganda. Television and radio programs, newspapers and magazines, described "Albanians" as a threat to the people and to the nation. The population was told that their jobs were at risk. Then the transmissions became a call to arms.

Edward Vuilliamy, a journalist for London's *The Guardian*, traveled to Bosnia and Herzegovina during the war in 1992 and was one of the first journalists who went into Bosnian concentration camps. Vuilliamy said the messages in the propaganda campaign by the Serbian government in Belgrade was "relentless and was very cogent and potent. It was a message of urgency, a threat to your people, to your nation, a call to arms, and, yes, a sort of instruction to go to war for your people…. It pushed and pushed. It was rather like a sort of hammer bashing on peoples' heads…'"[43]

WEAPONS OF MASS DISTRACTION

In Iran, from 2006 to 2009, President Mahmoud Ahmadinejad used the media to focus his citizens' dissatisfaction with his economic and political policies unto the Jewish people, the State of Israel, and America. He organized huge demonstrations for the masses to vent their anger and frustration. He said that there never was a Holocaust and then demanded that Israel be wiped off the map.

Today, in the Middle East, TV programs aimed at pre-schoolers use the old Nazi images of Jews to create hatred. They encourage pre-school children to become suicide bombers. The enemies they blow up could be Muslims who do not belong to their particular religious sect or Christians, Jews and people of other religions who do not share their Islamic or political ideology.

RE-EDUCATION ON THE RADIO

In Nazi Germany the process of transforming the Jew into "The Other" was accelerated when the radio stations, under control of the Nazis, broadcast antisemitic propaganda all the time. This continual preaching and hammering by the media worked to convince people that the Jews were not part of their society and deserved to be killed.[4]

Hitler's first and most important goal was the re-education of German youth. He wrote: "I will have no intellectual training. Knowledge is ruin to my young men. A violently active, dominating, brutal youth is what I am after."[6]

Hitler targeted children in the first grade. Primers were printed in comic book form using bright colors. The image of the ideal German was strong and beautiful compared to the twisted caricatures of Jewish people. The Nazi propagandists understood that they needed to use horrible looking stereotypes to induce fear of the Jews in the very young and ingrain them deeply with a hatred of Jews.

Once he was thrown out of school, sixth grader Ernest Michel heard German youth singing as they marched through the streets, *"Wenn das Judenblut von Messer spritzt, geht uns nochmal so gut."* ("When Jewish blood spurts from our knives, it goes well for us.")

THE DYNAMIC DUO: JACQUELINE MUREKATETE & DAVID GEWIRTZMAN

Today, there is an extraordinary duo, two complete opposites, who go from school to school, church to synagogue, civic group to community group, to teach people not to hate each other and that genocide must be stopped. What they have in common is that they are both survivors of genocide. Everything else is as different as can be.

He is, as Gewirtzman himself says, "an old, white Jewish man from Losice, Poland," a man who came to America, earned a college degree and became a successful pharmacist, rebuilding his family and his way of life. Murekatete is young and black, a survivor of the Rwandan genocide.

They each tell their harrowing, painful, personal testimonies. At one event, there were young children scattered in an audience of about 60 people, yet for two hours, everyone remained rapt, almost unmoving, until the two closed with a plea for people to speak out about the genocide in Darfur. They were given a standing ovation.

When the war came to Poland, David was a 10-year-old. He was in class when a German officer came in and ordered the teacher to give up his Jewish students. When the teacher remained silent, he was brutally attacked, and the officer said he would not stop the beating until the Jews were handed over. One student pointed at David, who bolted and escaped from the school.

Then came a day when he and his family were forced to move to a ghetto. They were freezing because they had to leave their own clothing and possessions behind when they were forced to vacate their homes. Soon disease spread and the dead filled the streets. Finally, the family found a compassionate farmer who hid them for two years in a pit under a pigsty. In July, 1944, after he and his family came out of hiding, they went back to Losice.

Out of the 8,000 Jewish people who had lived in his town, there were only 16 survivors. Realizing that there was no hope remaining, they abandoned Europe and came to America.

Today, Gewirtzman lives in Riverdale, New York and talks about his experiences during the Holocaust to kids in schools around New York City and its suburbs. This was not easy for him. It took a very long time for him to learn how to do it without breaking down, but he did it because he was compelled to keep the promise he made to those who were lost.

David suffered from severe survivor guilt, but continued his work, going it alone, for ten long, painful years. He, like other Holocaust survivors, never failed to touch people, to remind them of their own obligations to remember, commemorate and teach an end to hatred.

One day, soon after the terrorist attacks on September 11, 2001 he spoke at a high school in Queens, and a few days later, as usual, received letters from the students. This time there was one from Jacqueline Murekatete, a 16-year-old, and it knocked him for a loop. She wrote, in part:

A few times I have asked myself if there are two races in the world, human beings and human-like beings...I can't seem to understand why [some] human beings [can] commit such evil and others would never imagine such a thing...I have myself...gone through such experiences as you had. In 1994, there was genocide in my country, Rwanda...my ethnic group was the victim of genocide...I myself ended up losing my family, my parents, all my brothers and sisters...numerous relatives...At one time, I...like you, had the feeling of guilt for being alive... Why was I left?...I never really got an answer to that, but now I am grateful that I was left. Maybe I can make a difference in this world if I try, and maybe I can do my part in making sure that no other human being goes through the same experiences I did....*

The two decided to meet for lunch and spent eight hours together. Since then, they have been inseparable on the speaking circuit, sharing their compelling stories with anyone who would listen. They are on a mutual mission to change the world.

"People do not wake up and decide to kill their teachers and neighbors," says Jacqueline. "There are precedents: racism, discrimination, dehumanization, and marginalization. In Rwanda, people were taught, preached at, and made to believe that being a Tutsi was a crime deserving of death."

People can resist genocide, nonetheless, Murekatete said. "People always have the option to do the right thing," she pointed out, citing the Hutu family who hid her and her grandmother for as long as they could.

In her letter to David, Jacqueline wrote: "The most important lesson I learned from you was that as human beings we face an ugly disease—hate; and the only weapon we have against it is education. I will try my best to use this weapon in fighting this terrible disease."*

---

*From a letter Jacqueline reads at presentations.

*Visit http://www.righteouspictures.com/ to learn more.

CHAPTER EIGHT

MURDER BY MUSIC

Singer Sentenced to 15 Years in Prison for Incitement

One of Rwanda's most famous singers, Simon Bikindi, was convicted on 2 December 2008 for his direct and public incitement to commit genocide.

Charged by the International Criminal Tribunal for Rwanda, based in Arusha, Tanzania, Bikindi was sentenced for his role during the during the 1994 genocide in Rwanda.

Bikindi, who was also a sports ministry official and founded Rwanda's Irindiro Ballet, was arrested seven years ago in the Netherlands.

Although several of Bikindi's "hate songs" against Tutsis played a strong role in the genocide, Bikindi was not sentenced for his songs but for a speech he made from a vehicle equipped with a public address system, where he encouraged ethnic Hutus to kill Tutsis.

Prosecutors at the UN-backed tribunal had called for the singer to be given a life sentence.

**from the website,
http://www.freemuse.org/sw31145.asp**

Music and words are a powerful combination, especially when they are crafted to tell lies. Because Hitler knew music had a powerful affect on young people, he made sure that school curricula included specially-written music that furthered the ideals and policies of the Nazi Party. The Nazi Youth anthem, "*Es zittern die morschen Kuschen*" ("The Frail Bones Are Trembling"), attacked the elderly and celebrated the smashing of peace. *Deutschland erwache* ("Germany Awake!") warned the Germans about the Jews.*

In the U.S. today, the equivalent of Nazi music is produced by Prussian Blue — a "white power" band with blonde, blue-eyed twin sisters, Lamb and Lynx Gaede, and other punk neo-Nazi bands. David Duke, the former Ku Klux Klan leader and U.S. presidential candidate, uses these bands to attract support for his racist ideas and to entertain his followers. They sing the praises of Hitler's deputy, Rudolf Hess, and songs about the glorious Nazis to all-white crowds at neo-Nazi National Alliance festivals and at Holocaust-denial events. They salute Hitler with a *Sieg Heil!* as they sing. Their music reinforces the nihilistic and hate-soaked ideas already in the heads of those who are attracted to it.

---

*For the lyrics of these songs and their translation see: http://en.wikipedia.org/wiki/Songs_of_the_Third_Reich

TUNING IN TO MURDER

Name calling and dehumanization were also used in Rwanda. In 1994, Hutu militants slaughtered hundreds of thousands of Rwanda's minority Tutsis and moderate Hutus. The Rwandan Hutu government used the media to constantly call for the extermination of "Tutsi cockroaches."

Radio Milles Collines, the national radio station, dominated the country's airwaves during the 100 days of slaughter. DJs encouraged the death squads and coordinated their attacks by playing martial music and songs that dehumanized the Tutsis. The *New York Times* reported that killers sang songs filled with hate "as they hacked or beat to death hundreds of thousands of Tutsis with government-issued machetes and homemade nail-studded clubs."[1]

Neighbors, inspired by the propaganda and music, systematically killed people they had known for years. Even the children and babies were not spared. One woman sat on the banks of a river and chopped off the heads of hundreds of her neighbors.

SEX, DRUGS, & ROCK 'N ROLL

Many songs and images in Western popular culture promote ideals like promiscuous sex, denigration of women, and hatred of the other, while extolling drug use, crime, and other acts that diminish self-respect. The music industry that produces these negative message music videos makes billions of dollars a year for American corporations. These corporations, in turn, spend millions of dollars to promote this music, which in turn creates violence and hate because it sells. The corporations say they are only selling music. Tell that to Tupac Shakur and Biggie Smalls, two of the most popular rap/hip-hop artists who were shot dead because of rap music culture and the violent rivalry it encourages.

The culture created by the lies in the music affects the future by affecting the behavior of young people. Some of these songs try to convince kids that what is basically wrong is good for them.

We might assume that pleasure equals good and pleasure alone will allow us to live happily ever after. This is more complicated than it seems. The songs, movies, and TV shows tell us that having all the alcohol, drugs, food, TV, or sexual experiences we can handle is good for us.

But that is not so. Alcohol, drugs, food, TV, and sex have benefits. Some of these are already addictive. But, taken in extremes, they become addictions; they have negative consequences, including death. A drunk driver is very dangerous to himself and others. A drug addict fuels a lethal criminal underground economy while destroying his own body and his community. People who overeat or eat the wrong foods put their bodies at serious risk of heart attack, diabetes and stroke, among other diseases. TV and video game addiction results in stifled personal relationships and an unrealistic view of the world that hampers a person's way of relating to other people in a positive way. Promiscuous sexual behavior has many consequences, including destruction of self-esteem, the high risk of getting a serious sexually transmitted disease like AIDS, or creating high risk pregnancies and unwanted children, as well as death.

These behaviors strip us of our self-respect. If we have no self-respect, we cannot respect others. Disrespect is the first of many steps that can lead to genocide. No one wants to be "dissed." As New York DJ Ru Paul put it so succinctly in the 1990s: "If you don't love yourself, how you gonna' love someone else?" And if you love yourself, you love your community. If you love your community, you don't want to see it go down the drain.

As the ancient sage Hillel said, "Love your neighbor for he is like you."

SNITCHING CAN SAVE YOUR LIFE & COMMUNITY

Rap music today promotes "anti-snitching" as the golden rule of the urban experience. It is not "cool" to report crimes to the police or other authorities. Encouraged by the lyrics of some hip-hop music, young people refuse to become witnesses in court. As a result, criminals go free and come back to the neighborhood to cause more trouble — the community and its residents become their continued victims.

Children in this "anti-snitching" culture — urban and suburban — become easy targets since there is no one who can protect them from the predators around them. They can't talk about the drug dealers on the corner, or about who raped their sisters or mothers. If they know who killed the man at the Quick Mart or liquor store, they aren't talking. They don't want to "diss" the crook and die by snitching. When guns are used to settle differences and the rule of law is replaced by the laws of gang-bangers, everyone in the neighborhood is at risk of death.

News reports are filled with stories about brilliant students, good people and babies who are murdered, often by accident. The neighbors, the witnesses, good people, are too afraid to say who pulled the trigger — and so more people die.

This is a complicated situation. If you are dealing with really evil people, when you snitch, you and others can end up dead. The question is: Can you join with others to stop what's happening? Do you and others in your community have the will to try? There are no easy answers.

CELEBRITIES SING OUT

Music can also inspire resistance to evil and move masses to do good deeds. Bob Dylan, Pete Seeger, Joan Baez, Peter, Paul and Mary, and other folk singers in the 1960s and '70s used their music to mobilize the peace movement against the war in Vietnam.

whyshouldicareontheweb.com

"War," sung by Edwin Starr, "For What It's Worth" sung by Buffalo Springfield, "We Gotta Get Out of This Place," performed by Eric Burden and The Animals, were all inspirational songs to Americans serving in the jungles of Vietnam.

Images on the nightly news convinced Americans that the Vietnam War was pointless—56,000 Americans were dead. Americans didn't understand who or what the enemy was in Vietnam. In World War II, people felt that America was an avenging angel, out to kill those who would subjugate the world. But the uselessness and distance of the Vietnam War aroused people to protest. Led by celebrities, musicians and actors, as well as politicians and intellectuals, they sang out and spoke out against a policy that failed. At first the protestors were accused of treason and unpatriotic behavior, until they persuaded mainstream America to join them. And then something unexpected happened: America's leaders listened and the U.S. pulled out its troops.

FROM THE BOOBTUBE TO YOUTUBE

Some celebrities today have tried to use the media and their celebrity status to make the world a better place. One of the first to use television to raise funds for a worthy cause was actor/comedian Jerry Lewis. He invented the telethon, a TV fundraiser, in the 1950s. Over the last 60 years, he has raised more than a billion dollars for research to discover a cure for muscular dystrophy.

Jerry Lewis still does his thing on network TV. But most of today's socially active celebrities have blogs and websites. They post music videos with messages to youtube.com and other websites, to convince others to join in their causes.

When there was a two-year drought in Africa in the 1980s, the global music community joined together and created Band-Aid in the United Kingdom. It came to the States as "USA to Africa," to inspire people to help and to raise funds for African relief. Their song, "We Are the World," premiered on MTV amid much fanfare. Sung by many pop stars, it helped thousands. Other groups soon also chimed in. Farm Aid and Live Aid concerts spurred millions to give charity and to care about others, whether they were farmers suffering in the Midwest or people with AIDS.

Homeless people in America were helped with the millions of dollars raised by comedians Whoopi Goldberg, Robin Williams, and Billy Crystal on HBO with their telethon, "Comic Relief," a copycat fundraiser of "Comic Relief" in the U.K.

Today, Angelina Jolie, a Hollywood actress, is a UN Goodwill Ambassador and Bono, a rock musician with the group U2, works with government leaders and private citizens to improve the health and financial conditions of the impoverished in Africa. Bono even convinced George W. Bush to increase American aid to help Africans with AIDS, and performed at Barack Obama's Inauguration. Others impressed by such efforts have joined in. The Red Product Campaign sponsored by The Gap, an apparel company, gives a portion of every sale to groups that fight AIDS in Africa.

Russell Simmons, a music and fashion mogul, promotes ethnic understanding at the Foundation for Ethnic Understanding, Founded by Rabbi Marc Schneier of New York, this organization seeks to build interfaith and interracial ties. Grammy-award winner Miri ben Ari, an Israeli musician, does the same with her music video, "Symphony of Brotherhood."*

---

*http://www.youtube.com/watch?v=jfz1hJZPsxM

whyshouldicareontheweb.com

CHAPTER NINE

HEROES IN WAITING

❦

Courage is not the lack of fear.
It is acting in spite of it.

Mark Twain

❦

The Righteous who saved lives at the risk of their own, in Lithuania and Latvia, were not at the center of the Shoah but on its thin margins. But it is they who proved that we have an alternative, that we can escape from the abyss of genocidal events. Most of the rescuers cannot be painted in black or white either, but in different shades of grey, like all the rest of us.

Yehuda Bauer
"Reviewing the Holocaust Anew in Multiple Contexts"

Courage has many definitions. Ultimately, it is the ability to act despite fear. The challenge of courage is to confront the vicissitudes of life and decide to act in a moral and ethical way, though it may seem easier to go with the flow and do nothing. Sometimes one has to act in the blink of an eye; sometimes one has to think about it for quite some time. It is a decision one has to make.

We are not born with courage. We can develop the ethical underpinnings of courage by learning to care and act on behalf of others less fortunate than we are. Most good people are aware of that.

Sometimes courage means sacrificing something in order to do the right thing. This kind of courage is a rare quality. Yet all of us, regardless of who we are, can be heroes if we learn to be courageous. We can become pro-active on issues of morality and human rights.

SAINT OR SINNER?

Even criminals can act with courage and become heroes. Any person who has been irresponsible his/her entire life has a chance to redeem him or herself by doing good works. Regret and remorse are acknowledgements of misdeeds.

Oskar Schindler is the main character in Steven Spielberg's Academy Award-winning film *Schindler's List*. While based on a true story, Thomas Keneally's *Schindler's Ark* was categorized as fiction because, as he says, "I had written as a novelist, with a novelist's narrative pace and graphicness, though not in the sense of a fictionalizer."[1]

Schindler was real and hardly a role model. He was a thief, a braggart, a philanderer, and an alcoholic with questionable business ethics. He served time in jail and failed in business. He even joined the Nazi Party in 1939. Even so, he became one of the most famous heroes of the Holocaust.

In 1942, Schindler was in German-occupied Krakow, Poland, using Jewish slave labor in a factory confiscated from a Jew. (His Jewish slaves manufactured enamelware for the Germans.) With his wife in Germany, he spent his time in Krakow behaving like a playboy, hanging out with German officers, and providing them with wine, women, and money.

Schindler was friendly with the Nazis until he witnessed their atrocities against the Jews during a deportation from Krakow. His deeply buried sense of human decency suddenly surfaced. As a result, Schindler took responsibility for the lives of 1,100 Jews. He protected them from the Nazi death machine—even managing to extract Jews from the death camps. After the war, when Schindler fell on hard times, those he saved rescued him by supporting him financially. Some of them, who became real estate developers in the United States, would even name streets after him.

HARRY POTTER AS HOLOCAUST PARABLE

Harry Potter is an interesting fictional character, the story of a boy who was treated like an "other" and grows up to save the world.

To stop ultimate evil from destroying all that is ethical, caring, moral and decent, Harry Potter risks all in *The Deathly Hallows*, the last book in the popular series by J.K. Rowling.

His goal is to stop Voldemort, who is so feared and so evil that people call him "You-Know-Who."[2]

Voldemort was once a regular wizard but his greed and jealousy of other wizards caused him to make life choices that brought him to the Dark Arts and to evil ways. He hungered for power and became the epitome of the idea that absolute power corrupts absolutely. His final form was to be that of a snake — a symbol that brings us back to the lesson in the Garden of Eden — that we are responsible for who we are as individuals and as a people.

From the beginning of the *Harry Potter* series, Rowling shows how people begin to think of each other as "the other." At first, the "evil" is confined to the usual school antics, high jinks, and bullying, but there is something darker in the air.

As Harry moves through the years, the strength of that evil continues to grow, even as some wrongs are righted. The media, in the form of Rita Skeeter, the gossip columnist, begins to play into the story by spinning against heroes, turning them into villains, as politicians are held hostage by their own ideologies and by those who brought them to power.

In the early books, Harry is treated as an "other" by his own Muggle (people with no magical abilities) family. He doesn't understand why he is so different and why other people have visceral reactions to him — good and bad.

Dumbledore, headmaster of Hogwarts, the magic school Harry attends, becomes his mentor. From the day Harry arrives at school as a young boy, Dumbledore and others train him to use his skills to do what is right; to move away from the Dark Side and to fight it. They set his ethical standards, while they are increasingly confronted with growing evil being manifested by Voldemort.

Dumbledore sets an example of goodness and doing the right thing, and eventually gives his own life in an attempt to disable the Deathstick, the Wand of Destiny that would literally empower Voldemort and turn him into the vicious, purely evil snake he seeks to become.

As he gains power, Voldemort and his cronies, the Death Eaters, force Mudbloods, the children of Muggles and Wizards, to register at the Ministry of Magic because they are not racially pure. Then he sends them to Azbakan, a terrible place where they are guarded and oppressed by creatures that are called Dementors, who dehumanize them.

Muggles are considered by the Slytherin, Voldemort's minions, to be the vermin of the world. They eventually become victims of Voldemort's planned genocide. The book is filled with Voldemort's innocent victims, among them Harry's childhood friends.

In a life filled with secrets, Harry finally discovers the truth of his birth and how he has been used by those he respected and loved. Because of his disillusionment, Harry could have turned his back on the good people and allowed "You-Know-Who" to win. Yet Harry proceeds to fight Voldemort to the death, while thinking of those who died to protect him. Willing to die for what is right, Harry Potter, working with his loyal friends, saves his world.

Daniel Radcliffe was 10 years old when he began to play the role of Harry Potter in the film series. In an interview with James Lipton of the Actors Studio at Pace University, he discussed the role and the actors he worked with. At the end of the segment at the url below, in a scene from the movie *Goblet of Fire*, Harry talks about both sides of his character — the evil and the good.*

Harry's feelings touch us because all of us, in one way or another, we are just like him.

---

* http://www.youtube.com/watch?v=jtfeR4Sr_mo

MARCHING AGAINST SLAVERY & GENOCIDE

In March 2006, in the blogger's era, marching on Washington seemed like a quaint idea. But for ex-slave Simon Deng, the 300-mile Sudan Freedom Walk from U.N. headquarters to the U.S. Capitol, was anything but. It began on March 15 and ended on April 5, after he and his supporters marched through five states with stops in 19 cities.

As a reporter, Jeanette Friedman was assigned to cover Deng and met him on the Pulaski Skyway as he walked through New Jersey.

"In America," Deng said, "marching can make a difference," and this freedom is one of the reasons he came here to live. He was calling attention to the genocide in Darfur and southern Sudan and discovered that simply talking doesn't work. So he and those who walked with him took the message to the streets, hoping that Joe Average would see them, hear them, and act.

Deng is tall and strapping, a professional lifeguard who lives in New York. He is also a Roman Catholic from the Southern Sudan Shiluk tribe. When he was 9, a Muslim neighbor kidnapped him and three other Catholic boys and pirated them aboard a ship to Sudan. When it docked in Kosti, Deng was presented to his abductor's business associate as a gift. For three years he slept on straw and ate table scraps. He was told the way to relieve his suffering was to convert to Islam. He refused.

Then one day he recognized fellow tribesmen on the streets and told them his story. They rescued him and took him back to his father, who had given him up for dead. Deng became a champion swimmer and public figure, but was, for a very long time, ashamed to speak of his experiences. Finally, the unending violence forced him to speak out.

"America is a country where freedom is guaranteed," he said.

"So I am taking my anger to the State Department and the White House because they are playing cat and mouse. The [Sudanese] regime promised to help them against the terrorists, so the U.S. is not pressing them to give relief to the people of Darfur or to promote basic human rights. But Sudan is also not helping them with the terrorists."

Since 1953, Arab Muslims have killed more than 1 million African Christians and Muslims in Sudan, a death toll worse than Rwanda's. Since 2003, when the National Islamic Front took control, the violence went unnoticed as 350,000 to 400,000 people were killed in just 29 months.

Upset at the silence from the Catholic Church, Deng said quiet diplomacy doesn't work in the face of genocide. He said the Sudanese government provides arms and ammunition to roving gangs of Janjaweed Arab militias who, for a few dollars, will set fire to a village, rape the women, grab the children as slaves, and kill the men.

The Sudan Freedom Walk ended with a rally in Washington at the Capitol. Walking the 300-or-so miles to Washington from New York was not a challenge for Deng. When it was over he said,

> My people run for their lives and they don't train to do so. Back in Sudan, my people walk for months to get to a place for safety; they walk for months to get to a place where there is shelter; they walk for days and days to get to places and find there is no food. If they can walk, then why should I not do it here?*

When asked what kept him going, Deng said,

> I'm doing this from my heart. History tells us that when Stalin did what he did, people sat and did nothing and when Hitler did what he did in Auschwitz, people did nothing. My message is that atrocities are being committed and good people doing nothing tells the perpetrator to continue. When

---

*As stated in an interview with Jeanette Friedman, March 2006.

are we going to say 'Never Again' with respect to the people of Sudan? And more to the point, when will the international community ever act on the meaning of those words?

I ask this question as a victim of enslavement in Sudan; I ask it for my fellow Southern Sudanese who are always asking this question. My voice is their voice... We have endured and are enduring the most systematic destruction of a people since the Nazi Holocaust, but our fate seems largely invisible to the world.*

TORTURE AND TERROR

The question we must ask is not why heroes act in a courageous fashion but why there are so few of us who act with courage. Journalist Nicholas Kristof wrote about Dr. Halima Bashir in the *New York Times*.[3]

Dr. Bashir treated a group of girls between the ages of 7 and 13 who were sexually assaulted by the Arab Janjaweed militias at the behest of the government in Sudan. The Sudanese secret police arrested her, sexually assaulted her for days, and tortured her with knives while taunting her with racial epithets. One of her torturers told her, "Now you know what rape is, you black dog."

By the time Halima was released, her father had been murdered and her mother and brother were missing. England granted her temporary asylum and she was able to publish her memoir, *Tears of the Desert*.

Halima continues to be terrified of Sudanese retribution and knows that Sudanese agents are tracking her. Like Salman Rushdie, a moderate Muslim author who had death threats (*fatwahs*) issued against him by Islamic extremist religious leaders, Halima is living underground—in disguise, using a false name.

*As stated in an interview with Jeanette Friedman, March 2006.

When asked if she regretted standing up to the Sudanese and publicly decrying the genocide of her people, she said, "No. What happened to me happened to so many other Darfur women…. If I don't tell, all the other people don't get the chance — and I have the chance. I am a well-educated woman, so I can speak up and send a message to the world."

The courage and bravery exemplified by Dr. Bashir contrasts with the little that we, educated and well-to-do Americans, are doing about Darfur and other genocides and issues that affect all of humanity.

If victims come forward to speak, why do they stand alone? Like the masses who came forward in Berlin to support the Rosenstrasse protests, who will speak out with the victims of the Sudanese? Who will help the victims of Darfur stop the genocide of their people? Words are not enough, but they *are* powerful, and right now they are the only weapons the general public has at its disposal to stop senseless killing around the world.

RIGHTEOUS AMONG THE NATIONS

In *Conscience and Courage: Rescuers of Jews During the Holocaust*, Dr. Eva Fogelman makes the point that despite the different motivations for rescuing Jews, most of the rescuers had one thing in common: a tolerance and acceptance of people who were different than they were. This enabled them to continue to see Jews as human beings and thus not be swept away by Nazi propaganda. They were all willing to risk their lives to do the right thing.[4]

During World War II, residents of entire villages like Le Chambon-sur-Lignon in occupied France saved as many Jews as they could. Thousands of adult Jewish refugees found shelter and protection at church havens stretching from Poland to Belgium and France, Italy and the Balkans. Christian institutions also provided sanctuary for countless Jewish children whose parents were shipped to labor or death camps.

whyshouldicareontheweb.com

For example, when the Nazis swept Albania for its Jews, Bequir Qja, a Muslim resident of Tirana, hid his Jewish friend, Avram Eliasaf, in his tailor shop. When the Germans moved in, he took Eliasaf to a remote village in the mountains where, disguised as a shepherd, Eliasaf safely survived the war by masquerading as a Muslim.

We can only wonder in amazement at those few courageous persons who, risking their own lives and often those of their families and friends, saved a Jewish child, a Jewish friend, neighbor or stranger. Why did they choose humanity when their neighbors did not?

Saving a life could have taken a simple small act of caring and compassion—like handing someone a cup of water, or leaving them a slice of bread to find—or keeping a secret.

EDITH CORD: SAVED BY CATHOLICS AND JEWS

For a child in hiding, the challenges were enormous, especially for a young girl who had been sheltered from the world for most of her life. She was saved by people who allowed her to hide in plain sight, even in a Catholic convent. Though the Mother Superior knew her identity, few others there knew the truth. Here is her story.

Edith Mayer Cord was born in Vienna, Austria. In 1937, sensing the mood and changes in Austria, her family fled first to Italy and then, in 1939, to France. Her father and brother Kurt were arrested as enemy aliens and held in a POW camp. When they were released, they were each rearrested by the Vichy, the French government allied with the Germans, and deported to the Gurs concentration camp. Later, they were murdered in Auschwitz. Edith and her mother remained hidden in the primitive French farming village of Montlaur, where, before his final arrest, Kurt had made arrangements for them with the town's mayor.

Always in hiding, always hungry, always worried about being betrayed, she was but 15 when members of the the Jewish Underground appeared and told her mother that

Edith needed to be taken to a safer environment. Edith and her mother never learned how they were found, but soon arrangements were made and Edith was brought to the convent at Castlenaudary in Southern France. There, Edith Mayer disappeared. She was given a new name, Elise Maillet, with papers to match, and was asked to memorize her new "story."

My story was that my mother lived in Nice, my father was a POW, and I had no siblings. My parents were non-practicing Catholics, not uncommon in France.

I never forgot the date. It was July 3, 1943, two weeks after my 15th birthday. Soon after I got my papers and my story straight, a member of the Jewish resistance and I boarded a train for Castelnaudary. It was a nearby town of about 3,000 people, where a convent was located....As we traveled, I took out my new papers and examined them. That's when I noticed my thumb print was missing, a dangerous business. My guide quickly took out his fountain pen, and I put my thumb on the inkblot he created. Then I pressed my thumb onto the false document. My papers were then 'officially' complete.

I was fully aware of the dangers and was charged with adrenaline. I was petrified because I knew that my life was now in my own hands. I would have to lie constantly so as not to give myself away...I remember being afraid that I would not react properly when my new name was called.

To make matters worse, I was anything but self-reliant. I had never been separated from Mama, not even for a sleepover at a friend's house or camp experience, and I was utterly dependent on her. I knew absolutely nothing about Catholicism, even though I had always lived in Catholic countries...All this inexperience added to my stress.

...My guide left me at the convent door and I began my new life as just another Catholic high school student... I shared a room with four other girls. One of them, Naomi Zoe, was teased a lot because she was awkward and had a funny name. It wasn't vicious teasing, but it was constant and I was almost glad of that, as it deflected attention from me. I was trying hard to blend in and was careful to observe the other girls and imitate whatever they did when they prayed or crossed themselves.

...On my first Sunday at the convent, I noticed that there were fewer girls at breakfast. I automatically assumed they were allowed to sleep in because it was Sunday. After breakfast I went to church with all the students. I followed them to the altar and took communion, carefully mimicking their gestures — the folded hands, the downcast and pious look upon returning from communion, the silent prayer while kneeling at my bench.

...My action provoked an uproar with both the nuns and the girls. The nuns asked me if I had had my first communion. Of course I did not. Was I baptized? I said I didn't know. So the good nuns took it upon themselves to write to the priest in the village where I was supposedly born. The reply came two months later, and, of course, there was no record of me. Then the nuns asked me if I would be willing to take catechism. I said yes, all the while crossing my fingers mentally. I was prepared to do what I had to in order to survive. I was scheduled to start the catechism in September, with the new school year.

...Survival was a full-time job. I was constantly on my guard and had to screen every gesture, every utterance I made. I worried about giving myself away in my sleep. I had to be in the present at all times, to remember yesterday's lies and always be conscious of what I was saying or doing...

As school [that fall] was about to start, word came that I had been 'burned.' One of the students at the convent had relatives in Montlaur, and when she went home for vacation, she showed the class photo to her relatives. The person from Montlaur recognized me and told her my name was Edith Mayer, not Elise Maillet. My cover was blown and I had to leave the convent. I was gone the very next day.[5]

The Jewish Underground smuggled Edith to Switzerland, where she stayed until the war ended. Later, Edith moved with her mother to the French town of Toulouse, where she devoted herself to getting a university education, and did so in record time. Eventually, she immigrated to America, where she married and built a family of her own. She became a university professor and then a successful financial advisor.

A SPECIAL PLACE: LE CHAMBON-SUR-LIGNON

Hanne Hirsch was born in Karlsruhe, Germany in 1924. During the Depression she witnessed the Nazi rise to power living where she did near Socialist headquarters, a target of the Nazis. Political unrest seethed throughout the streets of the city.

The only normal aspect of Hanne's life was her relationship with her mother. Her father had died when she was but a few months old, and her older brother had left for the United States in 1937. Her mother supported them with a photography studio she'd inherited from her husband.

Hanne remembers Hitler's boycott of all Jewish businesses, but the studio income didn't suffer too much. They lost business from the city administration and a handful of non-Jewish customers, but in 1938, because of Nazi policy, people needed pictures for photo IDs and passports. Because there were no Xerox machines as yet, people also needed literal photocopies of documents. As a result, the business did quite well—until Hanne's mother was ordered to sell her business to a German. She preferred to close it down.

When the war broke out in 1939, curfews were placed on Jews. To further isolate them, telephones and radios were removed from Jewish homes. Then the Jews themselves were removed from their homes, as many Jewish families were evicted by their landlords. But Hanne, her paternal grandmother and mother managed to stay in their apartment. It wasn't long before they were joined by her mother's three sisters when they, too, were evicted from their homes.

On October 22, 1940, Hanne and her family and all the Jews in the provinces of Baden, the Palatinate and Saar were deported to France, to the notorious camp at Gurs.

In Gurs circumstances were different than in the camps in Poland and other countries. Relief agencies fought hard for the right to enter the camps and help the prisoners. The Œuvre de Secours Aux Enfants (Society for Rescuing Children, also known as the OSE—a Jewish French humanitarian agency dedicated to rescuing children), the Quakers, the YMCA, the Swiss Red Cross Children's Division and other Protestant and Catholic agencies were active there. Their main goal was to rescue the children trapped in the camps.

As it happened, the religious leader of Le Chambon-sur-Lignon, Pastor André Trocmé of the Reformed Church of France, had contacted the Quakers in Marseilles in 1940 and offered to help Jews held in detention camps. Together with his wife Magda, Pastor Edouard Theis and several local leaders, Trocmé convinced the villagers of Le Chambon to fight the German evil and aid "the people of the Bible."

One day, a social worker from OSE asked Hanne's mother if she would allow her to leave the confines of Gurs for Le Chambon-sur-Lignon in the mountains of southwest France. Offered a chance to save her daughter, she said yes. Some others accepted as well. Hanne and six additional teenagers were then taken by train to an obscure village in the countryside, where most of the inhabitants were Huguenot (Calvinist) Protestants. These were a people who knew what it meant to be persecuted for they had had their own history of hatred and intolerance during the Middle Ages. Though still under Vichy surveillance, Hanne enjoyed some semblance of a normal life among these caring villagers.

In the summer of 1942, through the intervention of participating social agencies, Hanne was permitted to visit Gurs to tend to her then ailing mother. Arrangements had been made for her to stay in the camp to care for her for a week, but when Hanne got there the camp was in lockdown. Two days later, about 1,000 inmates, including her mother, were deported to Auschwitz.

On the day of the deporation, Hanne got permission to go to the freight yards where the Jews of Gurs were being packed into cattle cars. By the time she got there, the train was already loaded. As the only civilian in the yards, she caught the eye of a policeman who noticed her standing alone, in despair. He asked her what she was doing there and she told him she was trying to find her mother. He said he would help, and he did. She and her mother were able to spend an hour together, knowing that it would be their last. Her mother told Hanne to go back to Le Chambon because it was the safest place for her to be.

When Hanne was originally sent to Gurs, she had met a teen-aged boy named Max Liebmann. Though only 16, Hanne knew that she had found her life's companion. In July 1942, Max was sent to a Jewish boy-scout farm near Lyon. Hanne stopped there on her way to visit her mother and later on the way back to Le Chambon.

About that time, rumors began to circulate about new Jewish roundups, so she told Max that if things started to happen he should escape to Le Chambon-sur-Lignon. Less than two weeks later, Max arrived. Hanne brought him to the Resistance, who spirited him away to a farm on the outskirts of the village. There he spent four weeks in a hayloft.

A few days later, Hanne and some other girls were forced to hide. In the dark of night they were smuggled out of the home in which they lived to the woods, where they stayed until nightfall. Guides came and brought them, two by two, to different farms, where they stayed hidden for four weeks.

When Max came back, he stayed in the village for one day, was given false papers and then sent on his way to smuggle himself into Switzerland. He made it on his second attempt. Hanne stayed in Le Chambon-sur-Lignon until February 1943. After her mother was deported, she decided she could not stay in France and wrote to her aunt in Switzerland saying she would love to visit her cousins. Though legal papers were arranged for her inside Switzerland, the problem was getting out of France. Without an exit visa, she needed to be smuggled in.

Hanne made the trip alone through German-occupied France, constantly in fear, always wary of anyone looking at her too closely. Her guide met her near the border and literally carried her over the Swiss border, which was a flowing stream. After spending the night at a seedy hotel, her aunt came and fetched her. As one of a very few, Hanne had been rescued from the German killing machine.

Hanne says no one really knows how many children and grown-ups were saved by the people of Le Chambon-sur-Lignon. As she says,

> We assume it was several thousand people, but we will never know because it was simply too dangerous to keep records. The people of Le Chambon-sur-Lignon are very special and have a moral compass that is not compromised. A friend who lives there recently sent me a note to let me know that the town has once again become a refuge for asylum seekers.*

As for the people of Le Chambon, in 1943 Pastor Trocmé was arrested by the Gestapo. Upon his release, he went into hiding, though he and his wife continued their rescue efforts. In April 1944, his nephew, Daniel Trocmé, a young manwho was headmaster of two schools in the area, was arrested for harboring Jewish childen. Although he could have saved himself, he chose to go with his charges. Attempts to save his life failed and he was killed in the gas chambers of Majdanek.

---

*Interview with Hanne Liebmann, May 2009.

In 1990, the State of Israel recognized all of the inhabitants of Le Chambon-sur-Lignon and those of nearby villages collectively as "Righteous Among the Nations." Since December 2007, the Israelis have also awarded many individuals from the town and its environs the designation of "Righteous." In January 2007, the French government honored the village's inhabitants at a ceremony in the Pantheon in Paris.

JEWS WHO RESCUED JEWS

Under the pressure of the Nazis, many people made terrible choices while others continued to maintain their humanity and decency. Where they could, many Jews used ingenuity to save other Jews.

One woman, Itka Grinberg-Ganot, a Polish Jew, saved hundreds of children and families when she set up a smuggling route between Bochnia, Poland and Budapest, Hungary. She accomplished what she could by "serving" the local Nazi commandant's wife as a dressmaker and cook. Like all the rest of those involved in rescue, her life was always at risk. After the Holocaust, she moved to Israel and was given an award for her rescue efforts.

HADASSAH BIMKO ROSENSAFT[6]

Before the war, Hadassah Bimko was a dental surgeon. During her incarceration in Auschwitz, where her son and husband were murdered, she served as a "medic" in the infirmary, using her skills to perform rudimentary surgery, camouflaging women's wounds, and sending the sick to work in advance of selections. If caught by the Germans, she would have been killed.

On November 14, 1944 SS Dr. Josef Mengele sent her and eight other Jewish women to Bergen-Belsen as a "medical team." There they took over a barrack for 149 Jewish children ranging in age from infancy to their teens, all but one of whom survived. That was far from Mengele's intention.

One of her fellow inmates, Hel Los Jafe, described how Hadassah "walked from block to block, found the children, took them, lived with them, and took care of them." After the war, when Golda Meir asked her how many of the survivors were normal, Hadassah replied, "We are all crazy because we are so normal."

Hadassah was also a principal witness for the prosecution at the first trial of Nazi war criminals before a British military tribunal held in Lüneburg, Germany. Then, in April 1946, she accompanied a group of Jewish orphans on a boat to Palestine, and saw them settled there.

After the war, Hadassah had the courage to remarry. Her new husband was Josef Rosensaft, chairman of the Central Committee of Liberated Jews in the British Zone. Their son Menachem, whose name means consolation, was born in the Bergen-Belsen cocentration camp, a place the family refused to leave until 1950, when all the displaced persons in the camp had been resettled.

SELF-EFFACING YET HEROIC: THE ABADIS[7]

In 1942 a young French couple, Moussa Abadi and Odette Rosenstock—Moussa, a Syrian-born Sorbonne professor, and Odette, a recent medical school graduate affected by the Gertman laws restricting Jewish medical practice—relocated from Paris to non-Vichy southern France. In Nice, which was under Italian occupation, with a background in acting and languages, Abadi was hired as a teacher in a Catholic theological seminary. In September 1943, after the Germans occupied the area and began deporting its Jews, Abadi decided to set up a network to save children. He asked for help from his employer, Monsignor Paul Remond, the Bishop of Nice. The Bishop gave him the title of superintendent of Catholic education. The signed letter of appointment enabled Abadi freedom of movement and access to Christian institutions in which he was able to hide children. The couple secured safe lodgings in convents and some private homes for 527 children, arranging for their expenses and necessary papers.

Odette was arrested by the French in 1944 and turned over to the Gestapo. She survived a brutal interrogation in Drancy without giving up any of the children or revealing the scope of their operation, and then sent to Auschwitz and subsequently to Bergen-Belsen. Moussa continued their efforts from hiding until the end of the war. At the conclusion of WWII, the reunited couple married and helped the children find surviving family members or, if that was not possible, find homes in orphanages.

Years later, now Archbishop Remond was recognized by the Israeli government as a "Righteous Gentile" for his participation in the Abadi rescue operation. As for the Abadis, the French government recently honored the memory of their bold and selfless work by renaming a site in the 12th arrondissement in Paris after them: "Place Moussa et Odette Abadi."

Self-effacing and never recognized for their work, it was only when Remond and other Christians were honored as righteous gentiles for their efforts in Abadi operations that the Abadis themselves came to be known.

HERO, VILLAIN OR BOTH?
RUDOLPH ISRAEL KASTNER

In May 1944, 12,000 Hungarian Jews a day were being deported to Auschwitz and murdered. Rudolf Israel Kastner, a Hungarian Jew, was head of the Hungarian Rescue Committee and one of the country's leading Zionists. He successfully negotiated the release of 1,684 Jews, including Jeanette Friedman's mother and other relatives. According to historian Yehuda Bauer, Kastner was also part of a confluence of events, including the need for laborers by Ernest Kaltenbrunner, the head of the Reich's Security Agency. That made it possible for 18,000 additional Hungarian Jews to be sent to the Strasshof labor camp in Austria, instead of being deported to Auschwitz.[8]

The deal entailed a Nazi demand for $2 million, forcing

Kastner to sell "seats" on the cattle car train to anyone who could pay. The Nazis also confiscated valuables from the passengers once they boarded the train.[9]

After leaving Budapest in cattle cars in June 1944 and being held hostage in the notorious Bergen-Belsen camp in Germany for some months, they were eventually taken by train to Basel, Switzerland in December 1944.

The idea of bribing Nazis to save Jews had originated with the Slovak Jewish Resistance—a rare alliance between Ultra-Orthodox Rabbi Michael Dov Ber Weissmandel and Zionist leader Gisi Fleischman, developer of the Europa Plan. The plan entailed using bribery to stop all deportations of European Jewry. In December 1942 Hitler had let his people know that such bribes were acceptable.[10]

In Slovakia, *Reichsführer* Heinrich Himmler, the second most powerful man in Nazi Germany, acted on his own. His explicit instructions were: "Take whatever you can from the Jews. Promise them whatever you want. What we will keep is another matter."[11] (Himmler oversaw all police and security forces, including the SS and Gestapo.)

Recha Sternbuch and her husband Isaac, were representatives in Switzerland of the Vaad Hatzalah (an organization founded in November 1939 by the Union of Orthodox Rabbis of the United States and Canada to rescue European Jews). With relatives prisoners of the Nazis in Theresienstadt, a notorious concentration camp in Czechoslovakia, they negotiated with the Nazis from November 1944 until April 7, 1945 through Dr. Jean-Marie Musy, the former president of Switzerland, and his son Benoit. These two prominent Swiss politicians were fascists and friends of Himmler's. As a result of those negotiations, Himmler released 1210 inmates from Theresienstadt as a gesture of goodwill.[12]

In the summer of 1942, Weissmandel and Fleischmann, who knew the Sternbuchs, bribed Dieter Wisliceny, an SS officer and Jewish affairs adviser to the government of Slovakia, with US$40,000-$50,000. Although the deportations to Slovakia stopped after the bribe was paid, there is no evidence that their payments were successful.[13]

After the invasion of Hungary in March 1944, Wisliceny presented a letter of introduction from Weissmandel to three Jewish leaders in Budapest, urging them to continue the negotiations that began with the Europa Plan.

This contact with Wisliceny led to the eventual rescue of 1,684 Jews on the Kastner Transport. The negotiations by the Nazis were spearheaded by SS Colonel Kurt Becher, an aide and confidant to Himmler. The deal also involved Adolf Eichmann.

After Becher collected the money, the train left Budapest. Then Eichmann increased his demand to include 250 tractors, with 40 tractors as a down payment. To pay for the 40 tractors, Recha Sternbuch needed 750,000SF (Swiss Francs) but only had 150,000SF. Saly Mayer of the Joint Distribution Committee (JDC) refused to pay the difference. As a result of that, as well as the Allied invasion of Normandy, instead of sending the train across Europe to a port city on the Mediterranean, Eichmann sent it to Bergen-Belsen, where the passengers were "kept on ice."

Eventually, Sternbuch managed to get a letter of credit for 10 tractors to appease the Nazis and, on August 21, 318 passengers on the Kastner Transport were released into Switzerland.

In 1952, while Kastner was working as a spokesman in the Ministry of Trade in Israel, a pamphlet written by Malchiel Gruenwald, whose family members were deported to Auschwitz, claimed that Kastner was personally responsible for the deaths of hundreds of thousands of Jews and was a Nazi collaborator. The Israeli Ministry of Justice sued Gruenwald for libel, but Kastner was condemned by the presiding judge for having "sold his soul to the devil."

He said Kastner saved only a "select" group of Jews by agreeing to keep quiet about the fate of the Jews. It also did not help that after the war Kastner wrote reference letters for SS Colonel Becher to advance his case at the Nuremberg War Crimes Trials.

As a result of all this adverse publicity, Kastner and his family were ostracized by the community. Kastner himself was assassinated on a street in Tel Aviv on March 3, 1957, a year before the verdict was overturned by the Israeli Supreme Court.

Did Kastner make a deal with the devil? Or was he a hero?

A FINAL NOTE

Roman Kent is a survivor from Auschwitz, chairman of the American Gathering of Jewish Holocaust Survivors and Their Descendants, president of The Jewish Foundation for the Righteous, chief negotiator for the Claims Conference of Jewish Material Claims Aginast Germany, and author of *Courage Was My Only Option*. When interviewed in New York's *Daily News*, he asked, "How do you describe a heroic act? [716]

"In Judaism we say, 'He who has saved one life, it is as if he has saved the world,' ... But the righteous gentiles did more than that. They risked their lives every day for years; they risked their families' lives. Heroism that could last for days, weeks, months and years ... we don't have a word to describe the longevity of such heroism."

Decency, Kent maintains, is not for the weak. "We like to teach people that anyone can be moral, even under the worst of circumstances — if they have the guts." [17]

*I*t takes money to make money, even begging.
Humans are herd animals. If a stranger's bleeding
to death beside the road, most people won't stop
to offer a Band-Aid. But get the ball rolling with
a couple Good Samaritans, and before you know
it you've got more eager philanthropists than you
know what to do with.

Sol Luckman
DNA scientist and author

CHAPTER TEN

THE BOLD & THE BRAVE

Even passivity was a form of resistance. To die with dignity was a form of resistance. To resist the demoralizing, brutalizing force of evil, to refuse to be reduced to the level of animals, to live through the torment, to outlive the tormentors, these, too, were acts of resistance. Merely to give a witness of these events in testimony was, in the end, a contribution to victory. Simply to survive was a victory of the human spirit.

Sir Martin Gilbert
The Holocaust: The Jewish Tragedy[1]

Sometimes doing the right thing is easy—like holding a door open for someone who has their hands full or helping people carry their groceries to their cars. On the other hand, sometimes doing the right thing can get you killed, especially when you live under a totalitarian dictatorship, without freedom of speech or religion, without work permits, without the ability to create social action movements. Under such circumstances, it becomes difficult to fight back against tyranny.

The Nazis were very clever at wearing their victims down, psychologically as well as physically. Collective punishment, the practice of making many people suffer for the actions of one person or a small group, was a basic operating procedure of German occupation that discouraged resistance of any sort.

At first, "Better to wait it out" was a common attitude among city Jews who didn't run to the countryside because they didn't know it well enough to survive. Nonetheless, many Jews resisted what the Nazis were doing to them, for they were determined not to lose their humanity and dignity no matter what.

Resistance took many forms in the ghettos, forests and camps. When schools were closed, underground schools were opened. When synagogues were closed, covert prayer groups were organized. Although no one was allowed to own a

printing press, there were 50 underground newspapers in the
Warsaw Ghetto alone. When food was scarce, soup kitchens
were opened; youth groups and political groups continued to
meet under the cloak of darkness. Jewish culture flourished
underground. Poetry was written; music was composed.
Theater performances were held in Vilna, Warsaw, and Lodz
despite the oppression, hunger and the threat of inevitable
death. Hope and faith mattered.

Jews resisted the Nazis whenever they could. From singing
songs or going into hiding; from blowing up trains to
studying the Bible and Talmud; by saving a life, by sharing
a meal, by putting on a play or a concert, or by sabotaging
the work they were doing in slave labor camps.

When the Jews realized what the Nazis really intended to do,
they took up arms knowing they could never win. They did
so as an act of defiance—to uphold their honor and avenge
the murder of their families. They knew they would die
trying, and most did.

They fought back in the ghettos, in the camps, and in forests
of Eastern Europe. And they fought in the armies of the Allies
and the Soviet Union.

THE PARTISANS

During World War II, partisans were the irregular forces,
detached light troops, and civilians fighting behind the
lines in Nazi-occupied countries. In France and Belgium,
where Jews were more widely accepted by their neighbors,
those who managed to join partisan groups were welcomed
as patriots by their fellow countrymen, with many of the
locals assisting them whenever and however they could.

In Central and Eastern Europe, on the other hand, especially
in Poland, many non-Jewish partisan groups were antisemitic
and would not allow Jews to join them. And so Jews had
to create their own groups. It was more difficult in Poland,

where 77 percent of the Jews lived in large cities, antisemitism was deep, and it was hard to find friendly groups who would hide them or help them survive.[2]

Usually, if you didn't already have a firearm, you could not join a resistance group, Jewish or otherwise. Dr. Yeheskel Atlas, a leader of a partisan group would ask every candidate before joining: "What do you want?" The answer he was looking for was, "To die fighting the enemy."[3]

Most partisan groups would not let families join because the cries of hidden children and infants could give away their positions. Miles Lerman, who came to America after the war and became a successful businessman and chairman of the United States Holocaust Memorial Council, said that he knew the partisans would accept him but "not my mother, not my sister and not her children."[4] Older people could not keep up. As a result, only 10,000 people survived in family units.

The best known group that protected families was the Bielski partisan unit in Byelorussia. The story is told in the film *Defiance*. Their leader, Tuvia, said: "Don't rush to fight and die…we need to save lives. To save a Jew is much more important than to kill a German."[5]

The tiny proportion of Jews who resisted were active in the cities and in the forests, doing what they could to fight the Germans and their collaborators. Many received help from Soviet troops, most often in the forests of eastern Poland and Lithuania. Some Jewish partisans were formerly in the Polish Army; some escaped from the labor and concentration camps; some fled before they could be deported. All told, it is estimated that there were between 20,000 and 30,000 Jewish partisans in Europe.

VILNIUS/VILNA

The call to arms in the Vilna Ghetto in Lithuania was a clear statement of the rage that motivated Jewish resistance.

Written by Abba Kovner, the statement was distributed on
January 1, 1942, just six months after the German invasion
of Poland.

> Jewish youth, do not believe those that are trying to
> deceive you. Out of 80,000 Jews in the "Jerusalem
> of Lithuania" [Vilna] only 20,000 are left. Before
> our eyes they took away our parents, our brothers
> and sisters. Where are the hundreds of men who
> were conscripted for labor? Where are the naked
> women and the children who were taken away from
> us on that dreadful night? Where are the Jews who
> were deported on Yom Kippur?
>
> And where are our own brethren from other
> ghettos?
>
> Of those taken through the gates of the ghetto not
> a single one has returned. All the Gestapo roads
> lead to Ponar [the forest seven miles outside the
> city], and Ponar means death.
>
> Ponar is not a concentration camp. They have all
> been shot there. Hitler plans to destroy all the Jews
> of Europe and the Jews of Lithuania have been
> chosen as the first line.
>
> We will not be led like sheep to the slaughter. True,
> we are weak and helpless, but the only response to
> the murderer is revolt!
>
> Brothers! It is better to die fighting like free men
> than to live at the mercy of the murderers. Arise!
> Arise with your last breath!

Michael Berenbaum noted that Abba Kovner's declaration
was written a full three weeks before the 1942 Wannsee
Conference that determined the procedures for genocide. He
writes that Kovner had already intuited that the Jews were
doomed. In his declaration there is recognition that Jews
were being taken to their deaths. The imagery he uses of

sheep to the slaughter is not the judgmental use of someone who was not there. The phrase is used by someone in the crucible; it is an ugly image used to stir up the people, to get them to revolt. But despite his strong language, it took 18 months before they realized he was correct.[6]

As Marek Edelman, a commander in the Warsaw Ghetto uprising said, resistance was not a choice between life and death, but a choice as to how to live until you died.

FACING FEAR & TAKING ACTION

The brave men and women, young and old, who fought back however they could, lived in every country in Europe, the Middle East and North Africa. They stood up, as individuals and in groups, against a mighty military-industrial system that was committed to murdering every Jew in Europe, and even the world.

Some of these resisters were small children, as young as 9, who acted as couriers, or young teens like Joe Kubryk, a street-smart 14-year-old who served with Russian partisans near Odessa.

Some left their homes with their parents, some with their parents' blessing. And some, like Joe, who were desperate to cling to life, had to sneak away, leaving their families behind without even saying good-bye, never to see them again.

Frank Blaichman was a 19-year-old who knew the lay of the land around Kamionka, Poland. To facilitate his family's survival, he never wore his Jewish star as he traveled from place to place on his bicycle, trading items for food. Had he been caught by the Nazis, he would have been shot.

The night before the liquidation of his ghetto, Frank said goodbye to his family. "I figured I would be dead in three days, but after I spent the second night with a friendly farmer named Glos, I decided I would be safer in the woods.

"I don't know how I made some of the decisions I made, but after I saw what was happening in the family camp in the forest, I thought we young people should build a bunker further away and be lookouts.

"We needed to make some rules and it saved our lives, because a few nights later, the Germans killed 75 people in the main camp. Later, when we were able to get some guns with the help of other Jewish partisans, we were able to take care of ourselves—and the German collaborators who led the Germans to our camp in the Bratnik Forest.

"We soon learned how to survive, and some people in our group, like Yankel Klerer, the man we chose as our commander, had been in the Polish Army. He trained us with sticks until we had guns."[7]

Blaichman survived the war. When the Russians came through Poland and attempted to conscript him, he escaped to the American Zone in Germany and emigrated to the United States. There he rebuilt his family in New York City and became a successful businessman and philanthropist.

THE PARTISANER HYMN

The most popular song of resistance, which fired people up and inspired them to resist spiritually and physically, was the "The Partisaner Hymn" by Hirsh Glik.

Glik was born in 1920 in Vilna, Lithuania, where he began to write poetry at age 13. When the Germans occupied Vilna in 1941, Glik was caught and sent to a labor camp. By happenstance he was sent back to the Vilna Ghetto, where he became active in the Underground. His song, "Zog Nit Keyn'mol," became the Underground's anthem. He died after being deported to Estonia, but his song lives on. It was hummed, played or sung in ghettos, concentration camps, in the forests, and wherever Jews gathered in Europe. Today, it is still sung at Holocaust commemorations and memorials around the world.

Never say that you are going your last way,
The lead-filled skies above blot out the blue of day
The hour for which we long will certainly appear
The earth shall thunder 'neath our tread
That we are here!

From land of green palm trees
to lands all white with snow
We are coming with our pain and with our woe
And where'er a spurt of our blood did drop
Our courage will again sprout from that spot.

For us the morning sun will radiate the day
And the enemy and past will fade away
But should the dawn delay or sunrise wait too long
Then let all future generations sing this song

This song was written with our blood and not with lead
This is no song of free birds flying overhead
But a people amid crumbling walls did stand
They stood and sang this song, with rifles held in hand.[8]

TALES OF HEROISM AND RESISTANCE
YAAKOV: ESCAPE FROM TREBLINKA[9]

Jeanette Friedman found this story about her uncle in The Warsaw
Ghetto Diary *written by Hillel Seidman, a journalist who lived
there. The entry was made in August 1942. In 1947, the diary was
published in Yiddish in Argentina. (Yiddish is a Jewish-based High
German dialect spoken around the world and written in Hebrew
letters.) It was later translated into English.*

Yaakov Rabinowicz lived in Warsaw, a vibrant, diverse
Jewish community of 400,000 people. By August 1942, when
this story takes place, they were all squeezed into the Warsaw
Ghetto, the largest ghetto in Poland. More than one third of
the population was forced to live in an area of 1.3 square
miles that was cut off from the rest of the city. People were
squeezed in nine to a single room. The area was surrounded

by a 11-foot wall with barbed-wire on top. Food, water, and
medicine were scarce. When people died of disease and
starvation, there were so many deaths that the burial societies
couldn't work fast enough collecting the bodies, so corpses
were left on the streets until they could be picked up.

Between July 23 and September 21, 1942, the Nazis deported
more than 265,000 Jews from Warsaw to Treblinka, a killing
center 60 miles away. Treblinka collected Jews from other
areas as well; approximately 5,000 Jews a day were murdered
there.

By April 1943, there were only about 60,000 Jews left in the
Warsaw Ghetto. The Jews rebelled on the second night of
Passover, April 19, and began a battle that raged into mid-
May. 13,000 Jews were killed. Then the Nazis deported the
remaining Jews and leveled the ghetto. Six hundred and
thirty-one bunkers used as hiding places were destroyed.
Ironically, this, the first urban uprising in German-occupied
Europe, with limited manpower and even fewer weapons,
lasted longer than the battles for Poland and other major
western and Central European countries.

Yaakov was a classic hero. He had choices. Once he escaped
from Treblinka, he could have changed his appearance and
gone into hiding. Instead, he risked his life to get back to the
Warsaw Ghetto to warn the people there about what was
going on in Treblinka. He believed Jews should die with
dignity, and urged everyone to fight for their lives.

When it all started for Yaakov, he was a 25-year-old Hasidic
(ultra-Orthodox) young man with "a fire in his eyes," who
came from a prominent family. His father had died before the
war. His mother ran a boarding house and house of prayer on
Gensia Street, in the heart of Warsaw's Jewish quarter. That
street, under the Nazis, would become the central avenue
of the ghetto.

One day, Yaakov, a Torah scholar and intellectual, was taken
to the *Umschlagplatz*, a large plaza near the railroad station,

and herded into a box car with almost 100 other Jews of all ages. They were packed in like sardines — like a subway car during rush hour. There was no toilet or water. Taken aback by the nightmare he was living, Yaakov took special notice of his surroundings and seared the details into his brain. In the dimness of the dank and jam-packed car, a toddler constantly demanded water. "*Peech, peech* [a drink, a drink]," it bleated quietly. But there was nothing to be had.

The stench of humanity and its frailties was unbearable in the dry heat, as were the cries and screams of those who were being shoved into other cattle cars. At one point, Yaakov raised himself up and looked through an opening, only to see Nazis beating and shooting Jews who didn't move fast enough.

The Jews of Warsaw didn't know where they were being shipped, but they knew it was not good. They were told that they were going to the East, ostensibly to work. Finally, the train began to move. Then it stopped. For interminable hours it sat on a siding. People fainted, became sick, and even died. The only relief came when the train was moving, and air carrying the scent of the fields surrounding Warsaw wafted over their heads through small holes in the walls of the cattle car.

Finally they arrived in a place full of noise, smoke, and barking dogs. The cattle car doors were unlocked and men in neat uniforms, with shiny boots and vicious whips, ordered them out: "*Schnell!*" "Fast!"

In the confusion and mad dash from the cattle cars, something made Yaakov hang back. Because he was one of the last into an anteroom where people were ordered to disrobe for their "disinfection" in the "showers," he was given an assignment to load clothing into the cattle car he had just vacated.

In anticipation of life, the doomed pushing into the showers had neatly folded their clothes and placed them on benches; some even managed to place scraps of paper with their names on their piles of clothing. Shoes were paired below—all kinds of shoes, slippers and dancing shoes, baby shoes and peasant boots.

Yaakov would later tell Seidman, "I fulfilled these commands like a mindless automaton, completely numb. I began by collecting footwear: girls shoes, children's shoes, men's shoes; ladies shoes, elegant shoes, expensive shoes; battered shoes; torn shoes; long tall boots. How many footsteps have these countless shoes traveled, tap-tapping, scurrying, rushing along life's highway until they reached this abrupt barrier?"

In the distance, from a building, shrieks and inhuman howls of agony ripped through the air. There was a constant unknown stench. A Pole, a political prisoner who was working with Yaakov and a few other stragglers, muttered to him: "My hair has turned white from hearing them. I have long wanted to escape from here, but it is not possible. While I am more used to these screams, they still intrude on my dreams." He then pointed to the building, and said, "From there, no one escapes alive. Ten thousand murdered is the daily toll, and it has been going on for weeks now."

Yaakov was suddenly seized by a will to live. He forgot about loading shoes and with superhuman strength feverishly began lugging as many clothes as he could to the train. Now he was rushing. A plan formed in his mind. He had to escape and get back to the Warsaw Ghetto to report what was happening in Treblinka. He said to the Pole, "That building should have a sign on it from Dante's *Inferno*, 'Abandon all hope, ye who enter here.'"

When the clothes were piled deeply enough in the interior of the fouled cattle car, Yaakov buried himself beneath them, risking suffocation. A German noticed he was missing and ordered a search.

Hiding under the clothing, Yaakov could feel those hunting for him tossing the bundles around, hoping he would give himself away. But he remained frozen, terrified of even breathing, lest he cough or move. Food, water, body waste, all of this was secondary to his survival. If he moved before the car pulled out of the death camp and someone saw the clothing shift, he would be finished.

For 24 hours he did not budge. He heard the wails and whimpers of his fellow workers when they, too, were slaughtered. Finally the train began to pull out. With relief flooding his senses, Yaakov worked his way out of the pile and freed his head and arms. His eyes watched the bright and lovely countryside flash by through the half-opened doors of the train.

When the train reached the outskirts of Warsaw, Yaakov jumped out and made his way back to the ghetto, to Hillel Seidman's office in the *Judenrat*. Seidman told him not to say anything to anyone until they had a chance to meet privately. When they met later that night, Yaakov told Seidman: "*Ich kim fin Dorten*. ("I come from there.)"

A fierce Yaakov told his story and then made his way to Emmanuel Ringleblum, another keeper of a Warsaw diary and a leader of the Warsaw Ghetto partisans. (There are records from Ringleblum's notes, found in a milk can in the bunkers of the ghetto, attesting to the meeting.)

Yaakov joined Ringleblum's ghetto fighters. Warsaw Ghetto survivors, like Adam Boren and Guta Sternbuch, reported that Yaakov made his way from bunker to bunker pleading with people to fight back, because he knew they were doomed. Like Marek Edelman, for Yaakov the choice was how to live until you are killed.

On the first night of the Warsaw Ghetto Uprising, the second night of Passover 1943, Yaakov was the first to volunteer to climb the ghetto wall. The Germans shot him that same night.*

---

*To learn more about the Warsaw Ghetto Uprising, visit www.gfh.org.il/eng/

*I*t's not denial. I'm just selective about the reality
I accept."

Bill Watterson
cartoonist, "Calvin and Hobbes"

CHAPTER ELEVEN

DENIAL IS NOT
A RIVER IN EGYPT

Denial contributes to genocide in at least two ways. First of all, genocide does not end with its last human victim; denial continues the process. But if such denial points to the past and the present, it also has implications for the future. For by absolving the perpetrators of past genocides from responsibility for their actions and by obscuring the reality of genocide as a widely practiced form of state policy in the modern world, denial may increase the risk of future outbreaks of genocidal killing.

Roger Smith, Eric Markusen
& Robert J. Lifton[1]

On the day of President Roosevelt's death, April 12, 1945, Generals Dwight D. Eisenhower, George Patton, and Omar Bradley arrived in Ohrdruf, a sub-camp of Buchenwald, a huge concentration camp with satellite slave labor camps.

Three days after the visit, Eisenhower, who would later become president of the United States, wrote to General George C. Marshall, "

> The things I saw beggar description... The visual evidence and the verbal testimony of starvation, cruelty and bestiality were...overpowering...I made the visit deliberately in order to be in a position to give first-hand evidence of these things if ever, in the future, there develops a tendency to charge these allegations merely to 'propaganda.'[2]

On April 15, 1945 Edward R. Murrow, the CBS reporter, gave the American radio audience a stunning matter-of-fact description of Buchenwald, of the piles of dead bodies so emaciated that those shot through the head had barely bled, and of those children who still lived, tattooed with numbers, whose ribs showed through their thin shirts. "I pray you to believe what I have said about Buchenwald," Murrow asked listeners. "I have reported what I saw and heard, but only part of it; for most of it I have no words." He added, "If I have

offended you by this rather mild account of Buchenwald, I
am not in the least sorry."*

FLYING IN THE FACE OF REALITY

It's astonishing that in this day and age there are people
who fly in the face of reality and deny the Holocaust.
The German government admits that Hitler and his
collaborators carried out genocide against the Jewish people,
and even today it continues to pay restitution to Holocaust
survivors. The Germans themselves memorialize the Jews
who were murdered and are preserving the historic sites.
On December 17, 1999, German President Johannes Rau
apologized to the Jewish people with these words, ..."What
they [survivors] want is for their suffering to be recognized
as suffering, and for the injustices done to them to be named
injustices... and, in the name of the German people, [I] beg
forgiveness."[3]

So why do Holocaust deniers say the Holocaust is a myth?

As Michael Shermer and Alex Grobman point out in *Denying
History: Who Says the Holocaust Never Happened and Why Do
They Say It?*, the deniers ignore the German government's
own admission of guilt and deny the blatant evidence.[4]

The Holocaust is the most fully documented, witnessed
and studied genocide in the history of mankind. The
impact on the knowledge we have gleaned from it is
multi-disciplinary — from medicine, science, business,
politics, religion, psychology, sociology, and technology
to almost everything we know and everything we do. Some of the
evidence is kept at the United States Holocaust Memorial Museum
in Washington, D.C., an institution created by an act of Congress.

Everything has in some way been touched by the Holocaust.
Some of the medical experiments were commissioned

---

*Listen to his report at http://www.youtube.com/watch?v
=wYVn0hzcSs0

by the company that makes Bayer aspirin. Synthetic fabric manufacturers, plastics manufacturers, computer companies like IBM's German-owned subsidiary, and drug companies—ITT, I.G. Farben, BMW, Mercedes Benz, BASF, and others—all played their parts during the Holocaust.

The Nazis kept meticulous records, and there are millions of Holocaust and slave labor related documents in Bad Arolsen, Germany, that are being digitized to make it easier to track those who disappeared. The records are not perfect, and sometimes things are impossible to find. Still, these documents are Nazi documents and prove the Holocaust did, indeed, take place. The Nazis even took pictures of what they did, and war crimes trials were held by the Germans themselves.

Many records are missing. Many were lost. People changed their names, or jumped from trains and never made it to their destinations. We do not know everything, but it bears repeating: We know more about the Holocaust than any other event in history.

"THE BIG LIE" IS BACK

What do the deniers say? How can they say it? Until fairly recently, they were able to say whatever they wanted to say under the rubric of "free speech." Among their statements are those that describe the Holocaust as a myth invented by the fictitious "Elders of Zion" described in the *Protocols* fabrication. According to them, the "Elders" want to advance the global interests of the Jews.

In Western countries, Holocaust denial is a continuation of the traditional racist, antisemitic canards refined by the Nazis. These racial theories and political views are embedded in denier culture and continue to promote racist ideology and traditional Jew-hatred using old-fashioned Nazi materials.

The deniers call what they are doing historical revisionism, as if they were legitimate historians using historiography to correct false claims. True revisionists are historians who correct the past to include new facts. Those who say the Holocaust didn't happen are not revisionists. They are Holocaust deniers and antisemites.

The David Irving libel case against historian Deborah Lipstadt, filed in England in 1996, is a perfect example of why deniers don't want to be labeled as such. In 1993, Lipstadt, a professor at Emory University in Atlanta, Georgia, wrote *Denying the Holocaust: The Growing Assault on Memory and Truth*. In it she called Irving a Holocaust denier. Irving insisted he was a historical revisionist.

As the best informed of all the deniers, Irving made his living lecturing at Holocaust denial conferences. In response to Lipstadt's charge, he filed suit against her and publisher Penguin Books in England—because of its more stringent level of accountability than in the U.S. As a "revisionist," he claimed that since she called him a "denier," he could no longer make a living. He also sued because she accused him of intentionally misinterpreting the evidence in order to make it fit his theories.

In America, when someone sues for libel, the burden of proof falls upon the plaintiff; the person complaining has to prove that the defendant lied about him or her. In England it is the reverse: libel laws require the defendant to prove his/her statements. In this case the defendants had to prove that in addition to providing evidence that Lipsatadt's statements were true, they also had to show that there was sufficient reason to believe what Lipstadt had claimed. In this case, they had to prove Irving was, indeed, a denier and that the Holocaust actually happened.[5]

The defense hired historians to examine everything Irving ever wrote, dissecting every word. Over a two-year period, they built a solid case by quoting everything Irving misrepresented about the Holocaust. They also proved he misused and misquoted documents.

Indeed, in his 350-page verdict, Judge Charles Gray determined that Irving was a denier and a "right-wing pro-Nazi polemicist" because he treated the historical evidence in a manner which fell far short of the standard to be expected of a conscientious historian. He "misrepresented and distorted the evidence which was available to him." It was also "incontrovertible" that "Irving qualifies as a Holocaust denier." His denial of the gas chambers and of the systematic and centrally directed nature of the mass shootings of Jews was "contrary to the evidence."

Later, Irving was jailed in Austria for promoting Holocaust denial, which falls under criminal statutes adopted by the European Union in April 2007. After his arrest in Austria, Irving claimed that he had since changed his opinions about the Holocaust and said, "I said that then based on my knowledge at the time, but by 1991 when I came across the Eichmann papers, I wasn't saying that anymore and I wouldn't say that now. The Nazis did murder millions of Jews."[6]

When she heard that David Irving was jailed in Austria, Lipstadt said she didn't believe in winning battles via censorship. The way to fight Holocaust deniers, she believes, is with history and with truth.

Historian Alex Grobman has a different view. "In Austria and Germany, the situation is different than in the United States. In these two European countries, Holocaust denial, Nazi symbols, literature and music are banned.[7]

"Hans-Ulrich Wehler, one of Germany's most esteemed historians, is quoted in *Der Spiegel* magazine as being in favor of Irving's incarceration. 'The Holocaust,' he said, 'is a matter of the industrially organized mass murder of six million human beings. And to brazenly deny this, in the peculiar manner of the current Iranian government, is unbearable, at least in the German public sphere.'"[8]

ELISABETH MEYNARD MAXWELL:
RIGHTEOUS GENTILE OF ANOTHER SORT[9]

Elisabeth (Betty) Meynard Maxwell is a descendent of French Kings, whose paternal side of the family had been Protestants since the Reformation. The Meynards lived in an 18th century residence with 20 rooms, a stone house typical of Southeastern France. In his youth, Betty's father inherited a million in gold and lost it all at the gaming tables, and later as an officer in the Great War (World War I), he'd carried on a correspondence with Mata Hari, the Paris dancer who became a German spy. Betty has the letters to prove it.

Betty's mother, Colomb Pentel, was a Catholic descendant of the Pentels who fought for the Republic in the French Revolution and lost relatives protecting the Pope in Rome. The crash of 1929 reduced the family's circumstances and forced them to move to Lyon, where Betty's mother established a boardinghouse and school while her husband looked for work. Betty was sent to a convent school in England and traveled back and forth across the Channel. During World War II, she worked as a teacher in a Paris boarding school and studied at the Sorbonne. It was an uncomfortable existence especially when her good looks attracted the attention of German officers.

Betty says it is unconscionable that she did not understand what was happening to the Jews then. Living with her parents in the *Marais*, the Jewish quarter of Paris, she realized the Jews were slowly disappearing. Some were denounced by their neighbors and others were betrayed by the guides who were to take them to unoccupied France.

She spent the summer of 1942 in unoccupied France unknowingly acting as a decoy while others trained to scuba dive for the Resistance. By the time she returned to Paris, all her Jewish neighbors were gone. Her father told her that on July 16 he had been threatened with being sent to one of "those" places for trying to stop the Germans from deporting 30 Jewish families who lived in the same apartment house as the Meynards. Those families were taken to the Velodrome d' Hiver, a cycling arena used as a staging platform, and sent to Gurs and Auschwitz. When allied troops liberated Paris and General Charles De Gaulle marched down the Champs Elysees, Betty was part of the cheering mob.

A week later, her pastor gave a sermon that recalled "the terrible price that had been paid to secure our freedom still being borne by the prisoners of war, political deportees, and Jewish deportees." It was a statement of thanksgiving and an appeal for tolerance — a warning against premature euphoria. As she listened to his words, Betty Meynard resolved to make a positive contribution. She joined the Welcome Committee for Allied Officers.

That's where Betty met her husband, the former Leibie Hoch, a kid who ran away from the Hasidic *shtetl* (village) he was born in and, after a series of adventures, including a stint in the French Foreign Legion, arrived in Paris as Battalion Sniper Sergeant Leslie Ivan du Maurier. He later earned a field commission for valor, joined the intelligence service, changed his name to Robert Maxwell and was awarded the Military Cross by Field Marshall Bernard Montgomery. After the war, Maxwell founded a prestigious academic and scientific British publishing house and later became a media mogul. Their life together was a difficult one, but Betty Maxwell was determined to make it work.

Along the way she made some discoveries about herself. She took an interest in family genealogy and, after a 1978 trip to Carpathia to her husband's *shtetl* Szlatina, discovered that not one of its 2,000 Jewish residents remained. Three generations of her husband's family were no more. As she said, "They'd gone up in smoke. Alas, literally."

All that remained were two of his sisters and a smattering of cousins. She began to trace his family with a base of 17 names. At first she was uncomfortable when talking to his family because she had not converted to Judaism when she married. When she discovered that some of his relatives had founded the Jewish

Family Genealogical Society, she worked with them and soon had hundreds of names.

> I decided to put a yellow Star of David next to the names of all the people that were murdered. The genealogical chart was folded like a concertina, and when it fell open what struck me was a rain of golden stars—all of them for 500 of my husband's closest relatives. That absolutely shook me. You cannot comprehend a number like six million but when you have the names…From that day I had to know what happened, though I had no idea of what I was going to do with this knowledge. I started studying deeply.

For five years Betty was obsessed with Holocaust studies, but not in a formal setting.

> The more you read, the more you understand. The more you understand, the more you want to read. It wasn't possible for me to remain the same Christian before Auschwitz as after Auschwitz because of the big part Christianity played in that catastrophe. Once you have accepted that, something has to change.
> As one person the only thing that you can do is go about teaching others. I decided I would never again be a bystander in my life. If I did not like something, I would speak out. It gave me enormous freedom.

Betty, who was initially in denial herself, has said that the silence of the world during the Holocaust was so widespread that, "being aware of it should make every Christian of my generation unable to look any Jew in the face."

In 1981 Betty began to lecture Church groups and others about the Holocaust. She became chairperson of the first international Holocaust conference, "Remembering For The Future," held at Oxford University in 1988. The second conference was held in Berlin in 1994 and the last was held at Oxford in 2000. She has since won many awards and received two honorary doctorates.

The week before she served as Marshall of the Israel Day Parade in New York City in 1996, she visited Yad LaYeled, the children's museum at The Ghetto Fighters' House in Israel, that memorializes the one and a half million children murdered in the Holocaust.

"Hardly have I recovered from remembering all those bright innocent children who disappeared in smoke when I find myself marching with the Mayor of New York, a band, majorettes and 28,000 children. Their banners and placards illustrated their theme, 'Milestones and Miracles.' The miracle is these children, many of them born into the families of survivors. Their parents and grandparents were the children who had willed themselves to live or had been saved through the love of parents and rescuers."

THE POPE AND HOLOCAUST DENIAL

In January 2009, the Vatican's Congregation for Bishops lifted the excommunication placed on four bishops of the Lefevbrist Society of St. Pius X. Pope Benedict lifted the ban in attempt to heal a 20-year-old schism that began when they were ordained without the permission of Pope John Paul II. The Lefevbrist society rejects the Vatican's teaching on religious freedom and pluralism, especially the *"Nostra Aetate."*

Just days before the ban was lifted, Richard Williamson, who headed a Lefevbrist seminary in Argentina, was interviewed on Swedish television and denied the Holocaust. He said that there were no gas chambers and that no more than 300,000 Jews died in concentration camps.

A public outcry was raised around the world and across religious denominations, especially among Catholics. Williamson apologized for the grief he caused the church, but not for his comments. His apology was rejected by the Vatican. German Chancellor Angela Merkel called on the Vatican to "clarify unambiguously that there can be no denial" that the Nazis killed six million Jews.

A statement from Pope Benedict XVI said that he had not been aware of Bishop Williamson's views at the time he revoked the excommunication. Williamson was removed as head of the seminary and expelled from Argentina. He went to England, and the German government is considering bringing him to trial for denying the Holocaust. Church leaders have made many statements against Holocaust denial in the storm's aftermath, but people wanted to hear it from the Pope himself. The Pope was born in Germany, was forced to join the Hitler Youth during the war, and later deserted the Wehrmacht (German armed forces). Jews in particular wanted him to speak out against Holocaust denial personally.

On a tension-filled trip to Israel in May 2009, where he sought to improve relations between the Abrahamic faiths for the sake of peace, Pope Benedict XVI met with Holocaust survivors at Yad Vashem. He lit the eternal flame and spoke movingly about never forgetting. As he was leaving the Holy Land, at the farewell ceremony, he said:

> Mr President, you and I planted an olive tree at your residence on the day that I arrived in Israel. The olive tree, as you know, is an image used by Saint Paul to describe the very close relations between Christians and Jews. Paul describes in his Letter to the Romans how the Church of the Gentiles is like a wild olive shoot, grafted onto the cultivated olive tree which is the People of the Covenant (cf. 11:17-24). We are nourished from the same spiritual roots. We meet as brothers, brothers who at times in our history have had a tense relationship, but now are firmly committed to building bridges of lasting friendship.

> "The ceremony at the Presidential Palace was followed by one of the most solemn moments of my stay in Israel—my visit to the Holocaust Memorial at Yad Vashem, where I paid my respects to the victims of the *Shoah*. There also I met some of the survivors. Those

deeply moving encounters brought back memories of my visit three years ago to the death camp at Auschwitz, where so many Jews — mothers, fathers, husbands, wives, sons, daughters, brothers, sisters, friends — were brutally exterminated under a godless regime that propagated an ideology of anti-Semitism and hatred. That appalling chapter of history must never be forgotten or denied. On the contrary, those dark memories should strengthen our determination to draw closer to one another as branches of the same olive tree, nourished from the same roots and united in brotherly love.[10]

NO HOLOCAUST, NO ISRAEL

The main premise behind the establishment of the State of Israel is that for 2000 years the Jews wandered and were victimized after they were exiled from their homeland in Palestine in 70 C.E. In the minds of many world leaders, the Holocaust was the culmination of 2000 years of setting one people apart and labeling them as "the Other," always there to be used as a scapegoat for the ills of society. History demonstrated that because the Jews had no government to protect them and no place to run to, they needed a place of their own.

In the aftermath of World War I, the victors divvied up the Middle East and created new countries, including Lebanon, Iran, Jordan, and Iraq. The Jews, too, were promised a country by means of the England's Balfour Declaration of 1917. Mandate Palestine — the amount of land designated as the Jewish homeland — was originally to reach Trans-Jordan and extend to the Mediterranean but shrank as Arab pressure on Britain increased.

The Jewish people, via the Jewish Agency, nevertheless agreed to accept a fraction of what was originally promised. Despite its small size, this land that dates its Jewish heritage from Abrahamic times, had always remained the spiritual center of world Jewry. But it took a second World War to

actually effect the creation of a Jewish state. With six million
Jewish dead weighing heavily on the world's conscience,
the United Nations recognized the state of Israel as the new
Jewish homeland. But no sooner was this recognition granted
than seven Arab nations declared war on the fledgling
country, a war they quickly lost.

Israel thus became the focal point of the deniers. If the
Holocaust didn't happen, then the Jews don't need a homeland,
and, according to the deniers (and anti-Zionist logic) Israel
has no reason to exist and should be dismantled.

THE MIDDLE EAST MUTATION

In the post-Holocaust world, Middle East deniers have
become the most aggressive. *The Protocols of the Elders of
Zion*, blood libels, and the accusation that Jews killed Jesus
are constantly spread through popular TV programs, music,
and in the classroom — even in pre-schools.

Why did extremist Islam pick up traditional Christian
antisemitism and Nazi propaganda to mutate into its own
genre of Holocaust denial?

For example, Islamic extremists use blood libel as an accusation
against the Jewish people. They say, as the Christians did, that
the Jews use the blood of innocent non-Jewish victims in their
ritual foods.

Since there is no Eucharist in Islam, haters invented a new
blood libel that said *Hamantaschen*, the fruit-filled pastries
Jews eat on the happy holiday of Purim, were made with the
blood of non-Jewish children. (Purim celebrates the Jews'
escape from genocide in the Persian Empire in the 6th century
B.C.E., in the area that is now Iran.)

The Bible specifically forbids Jews from ingesting blood. Thus,
it makes no theological or historical sense to say Jews do so.
Still, that does not stop the propagandists from spreading
nonsensical lies to create hatred.

For the radical Islamists who control most of the indigenous populations around Israel, Israel is a Western colonial power, a thorn of the West in the side of the East. Since it espouses a pro-Western culture, its presence in the Arab world spreads cultural ideas that shake up the status quo in Arab lands run by tribal autocrats.

Even before democracy, Israel brings too many modern ideas to the region, including freedom of the press, birth control, women's rights, and gay rights. The Arab lands around Israel are historically tribal areas, where religious chieftains rule in the old ways; where honor killings of females are not unusual; where gay men are executed by the authorities; and where family dynasties stay in political power because they are beholden to extremist religious leaders who control the masses.

TRIBALISM RULES

The Saudi royal family, for instance, is controlled by the Wahabi religious sect that inspired Al Qaeda, the terrorist group that attacked the United States on September 11, 2001. Fifteen of the 19 terrorists involved were from Saudi Arabia. The royals give the Wahabi religious leaders whatever they ask for, including billions of dollars to build their mosques and schools around the world. In return, the religious leaders prevent their followers from overthrowing the Saudi government, a major supplier of oil to the West.

Radical Islamic sects don't want people to think for themselves or speak out unless they are told what to say. The religious leaders want, and often get, total control of their people. In March 2002, Saudi newspapers reported that 15 young girls died in a school fire when religious police prevented them from leaving the building. They justified what they did by accusing the girls of not being properly dressed.[14]

Israeli and Western ideas are anathema to their thinking. The extremists believe that with Israel as the symbol of everything they abhor right in their midst, it must be destroyed like a cancer. That is why the president of Iran, Mahmoud Ahmadinejad; Imam Hassan Nasrallah, the Shiite leader in Southern Lebanon; Hamas leaders, Fatah leaders, Syrian leaders, and other radical Islamists say there never was a Holocaust. In fact, they stand the Holocaust on its head by making claims that the Jews are committing genocide against the Arabs.

REMEMBER

What these attempts at denial really are are attempts to negate the pain and erase the memories of Holocaust survivors whose primary directive is the word "*Zachor!*" "Remember!"

When the chief rabbi of England, Jonathan Sacks, visited Auschwitz with an interfaith delegation on the 70th anniversary of *Kristallnacht* in 2008, he said, "The Holocaust did not happen far away, in some distant time and in another kind of civilization. It happened in the heart of enlightened Europe in a country that prided itself on its art, its culture, its philosophy and ethics. However painful it is, we must learn what happened, that it may never happen again to anyone, whatever their color, culture or creed. We cannot change the past, but by remembering the past, we can change the future."[15]

In his April 2009 article for the Jerusalem Center for Public Affairs, Prof. Yehuda Bauer wrote: "Today for the first time since 1945, Jews are again threatened, openly, by a radical Islamic genocidal ideology whose murderous rantings must be taken more seriously than the Nazi ones were. The direct connection between World War II, the *Shoah*, and present-day genocidal events and threats is more than obvious. The

*You can listen to it at:
http://www.youtube.com/watch?v=yDxn7uolH7k

Shoah was unprecedented; but it was a precedent, and that precedent is in danger of being followed."[16]

For the Holocaust survivors and their descendants, "Never Again" means Never Again—not just for Jews, but for anyone! Perhaps Remedy of the rap group, Wu Tang Clan, said it best in his song, "Never Again."*

*S*urvival *is a privilege which entails obligations. I am forever asking myself what I can do for those who have not survived. The answer I have found for myself (and which need not necessarily be the answer for every survivor) is: I want to be their mouthpiece, I want to keep their memory alive, to make sure the dead live on in that memory.*[1]

Simon Wiesenthal
Justice Not Vengeance

CHAPTER TWELVE

STORIES OF SURVIVAL

A *person's stories belong to the future. That's how memories live on and your descendants remember you.*

Eta Wrobel
My Life, My Way

THE SPARROW: PESKA FRIEDMAN[1]

Peska Rabinowicz, the sister of the young man who escaped from Treblinka and died in the Warsaw Ghetto uprising (see Chapter 10), also has an interesting story to tell. It is a story of faith and good fortune...and of survival.

As the Nazis occupied Warsaw, their mother, Yitta, the female head of the Rabinowicz family, collected more than 100 Torah scrolls and kept them in her dining room for safekeeping. Her home also became a refuge for the starving and sick.

Of her many children, two had died before the war, two of her children and their families were murdered by the Nazis. four escaped to Hungary, Palestine, and Siberia, and Peska and Yaakov were in the ghetto. After October 2, 1940, when their third floor apartment was incorporated into the ghetto, her mother insisted that Peska, then 19, escape. Her brother Baruch, a famous rabbi in Munkacs (now in Ukraine), made the arrangements and begged his mother to leave as well. But Yitta said that her fate was linked to that of the Torah scrolls. She would not abandon them. (She later died of typhus and had the last formal funeral held for a Jew in Warsaw.)

In the meantime, the Nazis were tightening their hold on the Jews and had started deportations. Each day conditions in the ghetto grew worse. Yitta begged her daughter to leave. But Peska did not want to leave her beloved mother behind, and even if she agreed, there was no one to lead her out of the ghetto. A sheltered, inexperience young girl, it was impossible for her to undertake such action by herself.

Then, one day, a man sent by Baruch came and promised Yitta that he could smuggle Peska to a family in Nowy Targ, approximately 150 miles away. She was to pose as his wife until they got there, but if he was stopped and questioned, he would leave her to her own devices. Despite the dreaded risks and with no papers, Peska decided to leave.

Before she left, the young, deeply religious girl promised her mother three things. If she survived and married, she would remain an observant Jew and would wear a wig in the family tradition. She would write the book her mother insisted she write—in order to bear witness. (*Going Forward* became that book). The final promise to Yitta was that on this journey, Peska would not look back or retrace her steps. She would only go forward.

Peska took a coat made for her from her late father's big fur coat; a tube of toothpaste; a single change of clothes, and three books which later became too dangerous to own: a prayer book, a book of Psalms and one of Yiddish poetry.

After a few weeks of hiding in Nowy Targ, where conditions were not as perilous as those in Warsaw, Peska took the bus to the Slovakian border. She threw away her books so that they wouldn't give her away. With no identification or work papers, no money, and no guide, trembling with fear she climbed aboard a bus and sat down in the back. When they got to the border, the police asked everyone for their papers—except her.

Once she got to the Slovakian border, she was met by another of her brother's friends who brought her to Kaismark. After spending a few weeks there with a family, a hired guide led Peska through a series of nameless villages, where she stayed with Christian strangers. The teenager had no idea where she was or who they were.

Though she was terrified and had no idea what would happen next, she hung on to her faith that God would see her through her odyssey.

One day, just before dawn, Peska was brought to a Polish family in another nameless town and taken immediately to a hidden room. After eating some very greasy food, she became violently ill and needed to use the privy in the field behind the house. Disguised to resemble an old woman so that she wouldn't be recognized, Peska was shocked when she walked outside and realized that the entire town was filled with Nazi troops taking over people's houses and confiscating everything in sight.

If this Polish family was found hiding a Jewish girl in their closet, they would all be shot immediately! Peska was sure her escape was doomed. But her good fortune continued. A few days later, a note was passed to her with instructions to take an empty pill bottle and walk down a road toward the town pharmacy. The note included a license plate number of a car. Her instructions were to go to a certain intersection where she would find a man fixing his tire.

On the following Saturday morning, as instructed, Peska took her little suitcase and the pill bottle and embarked on what she hoped was the last leg of her journey. She found her way through unfamiliar streets to the assigned road. On the way, a carload of SS men stopped to flirt with her, but she shook her head no and kept on walking. They didn't even ask for her papers! Then an SS officer stopped and offered her a ride. Again she refused, and again she was left alone. Finally Peska saw a car broken down on the side of the road. But the license plate did not match the number she was given! What could she do? She decided that because of her promise to her mother, she would not retrace her steps. And so she continued walking. But the day would soon come to an end, and the curfew hour approached when everyone had to be off the streets.

By now, Peska was well out of town. With fear and trembling, she prayed to God for a sign, for some indication of what she should do. Should she go into the woods? Should she continue walking along the road? If she made the wrong decision, she would be dead by morning. What should she do?

Peska prayed fervently for guidance from God. She knew that making the wrong decision would be dangerous to all who had helped her until that moment. If she was caught, the Gestapo might torture her as they tortured others, and she didn't want to betray those who had saved her life thus far. She pleaded with God. "Help me!" she begged. "Please, please, give me a sign so I know what to do!"

The forest at the edge of the road grew darker as afternoon turned to dusk. The birds were singing in their trees, when, just as she was about to give up hope, one little gray bird flew out of the woods and circled her head. She didn't know what to make of it. The bird it circled her again and then landed at her feet — and stayed with her.

Peska suddenly felt a chill come over her. Years later, she described to her children what happened next.

"The little bird flew down, a sparrow, I think it was. It flew around me and around me and around me. And from this feeling I had, I knew that this little sparrow was the sign from God. I said to God that whatever the sparrow would do, I would do. If it went into the woods, I would hide in the woods. If it went down the road, away from the town, I would follow it in that direction. Wherever the bird would lead me, as a messenger from God, I would do what it showed me to do.

"The sparrow landed at my feet and began to hop back toward the town. I could not believe it. I had sworn I would never retrace my steps, but the bird kept hopping back toward the town. Not once, not twice, but three times. The sparrow stayed with me for at least five minutes, hopping alongside my feet, and did not leave until I began walking back in the direction from which I had come. When the bird was sure I was heading back to the town, it flew off."

Peska couldn't find the safe house for the longest time. Then she remembered a blue lace curtain in the window that caught her eye when she had gone to the privy behind the house. She began to search for a house that had a window with a blue curtain.

When she finally found the place, she knocked on the door. Her rescuer opened it and fell into a dead faint at her feet. The woman's husband dragged Peska back to the secret room and told her that five to ten minutes after she'd gone to meet the car, another note had arrived warning Peska not to venture out that day. There was a trap on the road and it wasn't safe. His wife had fainted because she thought Peska had been caught and that all was lost. Amazingly, that wasn't so.

The following week, another note arrived with a new set of instructions for Peska. This time Peska met the man with the car on a different road. He brought her to the Hungarian border, where her brother's friend, Volvie Friedman, met her. Eventually, she was smuggled to Budapest and put on the Kastner Transport and brought to freedom in Basel, Switzerland. Soon after that, Peska went to Palestine.

Peska uses the Hebrew word for faith, *emunah*, and says it saved her life numerous times—during the war and after. "The truth," she says, "is that my entire escape was a huge gamble. But so was staying in the ghetto. The only difference was that staying in the ghetto was a passive gamble and escaping was to take action. I preferred to be active rather than passive."

Eventually, Peska married Volvie Friedman in Paris. She came to the United States with her husband, had four children, and together they helped build an Orthodox/observant Jewish community in Brooklyn, New York.

THE POWER OF THE PEN:
ERNEST W. MICHEL[3]

When Ernie Michel was 13 years old, he was kicked out of school in his hometown of Mannheim, Germany for being Jewish. As a result, Ernie never made it past the 6th grade. Then two years later, on the night of November 9, 1938, the German government sanctioned the first official acts of physical violence against Jewish people and burned their synagogues, looted their shops and homes, breaking windows everywhere.

Ernie was in a suburb that night and watched the local synagogue burn to ash as everyone stood and watched. That night he barely escaped being arrested by the Gestapo. Grabbing the first train back to Mannheim, he found that his father, a tobacconist whose cigar factory was confiscated by the Nazis, had been arrested and beaten. He came home two days later, a broken man.

Ernie and his family were no strangers to discrimination. He and his sister Lotte had been expelled from school as a result of the Nuremberg Laws that discriminated against Jews. All his old friends shunned him. Yet in the spring of 1939, because he had nothing to do, his father insisted that he study calligraphy, the art of handwriting. Ernie couldn't understand, but his father was adamant. He told his son: "You never know when it might come in handy, and in the meantime, it will keep you busy."

Though Ernie had an American affidavit, arranged for him by a non-Jew in the States, his immigration number wasn't scheduled to come up until 1942, when it would be too late to save him. Having an affidavit meant someone in America was ready to take care of him, and that he wouldn't become the responsibility of the American government. The problem was that there was a quota system in place designed to curtail immigration. Eventually, Lotte was saved by Catholic nuns and was smuggled into Palestine.

On September 3, 1939, the Gestapo arrested Ernie. Pressed into slave labor at a nobleman's estate near Berlin, he was able to keep in touch with his parents until they were deported to Gurs, the concentration camp in France. Later, he learned, they were murdered in Auschwitz in September 1942.

In the meantime, Ernie and a team of 100 boys and girls were sent from the estate to the city of Paderborn, where for a year they were slaves shoveling sewage, doing jobs no other humans could bear to do. In February 1943, they were put into cattle cars and sent on a journey for five days and nights. People died of hunger and thirst but the Nazis only stopped the train when they wanted to know who had thrown a postcard out the window. A young boy stepped forward to claim responsibility. The Nazis shot him on the spot.

In March 1943, Ernie and his fellow passengers, all swollen with thirst and hunger, awoke to harsh sounds. They were brutally welcomed to Auschwitz, the death camp. The luckier Jews went through the selection process, where a doctor at the head of the line chose who lived to work and who was sent to the gas chambers. Those chosen to work had numbers tattooed on their arms and were absorbed into the Auschwitz slave labor system. For the others, it was their last day on earth.

Ernie was one of the lucky ones — he was chosen to live, albeit yet again as a slave laborer. Ernie and some of his fellow survivors from Paderborn were assigned to build the rubber factory at Auschwitz-Buna, a division of I.G. Farben. One of the first things he and his friends learned was that if you were injured or ill you had to avoid the infirmary, because it meant you would be selected to go to the gas chambers, a one-way ticket to the next world.

In the summer of 1943, a Nazi guard called Ernie lazy and hit him in the head with his rifle butt. Ernie was knocked out; a bleeding gash on his scalp attested to the severity of the blow. After a few days he developed an infection and had a splitting headache and could barely work. Though his friends covered for him, it was only a matter of time before his condition would be discovered. So, half-dead, he consented to go to the infirmary, where he knew his chances of survival were slim to none.

A guard directed him to a barracks where world famous doctors, imprisoned by the Nazis, were doing the best they could to treat their patients. Ernie simply wanted to have his wound cleaned quickly so that he could go back to his working group, but he discovered that he had to wait his turn.

After more than an hour, an important prisoner, Stefan Heyman, walked into the waiting area and asked if anyone there had a legible handwriting. Ernie hesitated for a moment, wondering if there was a catch. But as the man turned to leave, he raised his hand and said, "I do." By that time Ernie felt he had nothing to lose. Perhaps they would give him an extra piece of bread in exchange for his work. "I studied calligraphy at home," he said to the man.

Heyman stared at him and led him to another room, where he handed Ernie a pen and a piece of paper.

"Write down the name, the Auschwitz number and the word *Koerperschwaeche* (weakness of the body) and *Herzansshlag* (heart attack)." He watched for a few moments as Ernie relearned how to hold a pen and began writing the words he was ordered to write. Then Heyman said, "You'll do."

Before he began his task, Ernie pointed to his wound and asked if he could get some help. Within minutes, his head was cleaned and bandaged.

Ernie made lists and realized that he was writing down the names of those who had died of starvation, exposure, and disease. He also made lists of those who were murdered in the gas chambers.

Two hours later, Heyman brought him food to eat and offered him a permanent job as a clerk. After a few days of rest, during which time Heyman protected him from the selections where the Nazis would pick who lived and who died, Ernie went to work as an orderly in the infirmary. While there he was given extra food and helped save many lives by bringing some of the extra food he received to people he knew were starving.

Two years later, after being a slave in a number of camps, including Auschwitz-Buna, Ernie went on a death march that began with 60,000 people on January 18, 1945 and ended in Buchenwald. (Toward the end of the war, the Germans developed the technique of marching prisoners long distances from one location to another. Under brutal conditions, many died along the way — intentionally so.) He was sent on another death march, this one from Berga and escaped with two of his friends in April 1945.

After the war, he made his way back to Mannheim, where he was taken under the wing of Rabbi Abraham Haselkorn, a chaplain in the U.S. Army. Haselkorn introduced him to Lt. Al Hutler, an American officer who worked with Displaced Persons (DPs) in that region. Through Hutler, Ernie found a childhood friend, located his sister in Israel, and eventually became a correspondent for DANA, the German news agency, where he was assigned to cover the Nuremberg War Crimes Trials. Afterward, Ernie came to New York aboard the *USS Marine Flasher*, one of the first Holocaust survivors to come to the United States in 1946.

He began his American life as a journalist in Port Huron, Michigan, and then became a fundraiser for United Jewish Appeal. Working with his colleagues at UJA, they raised money for Israel and Jewish causes. Eventually he became executive vice-president of UJA/FedNY, one of the largest charitable organizations in the world. Although retired, he retains his title in an honorary position and goes to work as a volunteer every day.

When he wrote his book, *Promises to Keep*, he gave all the

profits to charity and was awarded honorary doctorates from Lehman College of the City University of New York and Yeshiva University.

While in Auschwitz, Ernie and his friends conceived of the idea that ultimately became the World Gathering of Jewish Holocaust Survivors in Jerusalem in June 1981. This event gave voice to the Holocaust survivors and their families, who have taught the world to remember so that genocides should never happen again.

A SON TELLS HIS MOTHER'S STORY
HELEN WEISZ

Helen Weisz, author David Gold's mother, lived in Dolha, a small town of 4,000 inhabitants on the banks of the Borzshava River in Sub-Carpathian Ruthenia. On one day it was part of the Austro-Hungarian Empire, then it was part of Czechoslovakia, and then it was part of the Hungarian Empire. Today, Dolha is in Ukraine.

Dolha was not very different from many small towns and villages inhabited by Jews across Europe. Most of the 120 Jewish families in the town made their living in trades and small businesses. There were two doctors, a pharmacy, a Ruthenian School, a Czechoslovakian school, and a traditional Jewish school called a *cheder*. It was also home to Ruthenians, Hungarians, Schwabians, and Gypsies.

In 1939, Dolha came under Hungarian authority, and the Hungarians passed restrictions on Jews that were based on the Nuremberg Laws. Jewish businesses were confiscated, Jewish jobs were lost, and Jewish men and boys were pressed into slave labor. It did not matter that Helen's maternal grandfather and many other Jews were loyal citizens who fought for the Austro-Hungarian Empire during World War I.

Choked off from any source of livelihood, the Jewish community was impoverished and began to starve. On April 29, 1944, Hungarian gendarmes forced the entire Jewish population of Dolha out of their homes and deported them by train to Beregszaz, where they were imprisoned in a brick factory.

As the Jews left Dolha, their former neighbors and "friends" taunted them and scorned them as they were being led to the train station. They could hardly wait to pillage their neighbors' homes.

Trapped in the brick factory, the prisoners (who had no food, water or sanitary facilities) had no idea what was yet to come. On the morning of deportation to Auschwitz, Helen's father, David, awoke to find that overnight he had grown streaks of white in his hair. He instructed his wife Malka to make sure that Helen was dressed in a way that would make her look older than her 13 years. He also told Helen that she would be the sole survivor of her family, which consisted of 11 souls, including her grandparents on both sides.

His advice was well-taken and saved her life. After a three-day journey in a packed cattle car, she arrived in Auschwitz on May 18, 1944. As the "passengers" were forced off the train, SS guards shouted, dogs barked, whips snapped, and rifle barrels hit people as they were pushed into line. Helen left the cattle car holding her little brother in her arms, but her cousins quickly took him away — a woman who held a child was doomed.

At the head of the line stood Dr. Josef Mengele, the notorious doctor of death, who chose who would live and who would die by sending people to the right or to the left; to the left meant death, to the right meant slave labor. Helen's two brothers (Mordechai Isaac and Ezriel Hirsch) and her two sisters (Yocheved and Sheyndl), her parents and all her grandparents were sent to the left. Helen was sent to the right. Within a few hours, except for 64 young people (including Helen), the entire Jewish community of Dolha had vanished in a plume of smoke.

When the survivors of the selection entered Auschwitz, they were disinfected in cold showers and were handed ragged clothes and wooden clogs to wear. Though it had been standard procedure, the Germans were now no longer tattooing numbers on inmates' arms. But Helen's head was shaved and she was sent to a wooden barrack where she and 13 other girls waited for another selection. There, they all slept together in nine square feet of space.

Surviving each day in Auschwitz was a miracle. Even the tiniest act could make the difference between life and death. Having a pair of shoes that fit or an extra piece of bread could make all the difference.

As it happened, Helen's wooden clogs did not fit and were causing her feet to blister and swell. A cousin who had also survived the selection found her a pair of leather shoes. Another time, one of her father's former students was also in the camp and gave her some extra food. With food so scarce, hunger constantly gnawed at her belly. Once, when looking for food, they went to steal what they thought were cabbages and found instead piles of decapitated heads.

After six weeks of constant terror and hunger, Helen was selected to join a work detail and sent to Geislingen, a sub-camp of the Natzweiler-Struthof concentration camp near Stuttgart, Germany. The main camp was located in Alsace in France and consisted of a network of more than 70 labor camps. The main camp was one of the places where inmates were used for medical experiments by Nazi professors from the Reich University of Strasbourg.

Geislingen was set up in 1942 to provide labor for SS contracts with private companies, in this instance the Württemberg Metal Goods Factory (Württembergische Metallwarenfabrik AG) for the production of ammunition, machine guns, airplane engines, and tail units.

After the morning roll call in which you were forced to stand for hours in snow and rain, the first of two shifts began. The work was divided into two 12-hour shifts starting at six in the morning. For over ten months Helen was a prisoner in Geislingen, and operated a stamping machine that made parts for machine guns. She slept in a room without heat and worked in an ice-cold factory. Forced to go barefoot in the cold, her feet froze and she also contracted typhus.

That did not stop Helen and the other women in the camp from sabotaging the munitions they produced so that the bullets or guns would not work properly. If they were caught, they could be executed. As it was, the guards often threatened them and beat them. Just receiving an extra piece of bread or an apple from a non-Jewish laborer was cause for flogging. Because of this, for many years after the war, Helen had night terrors and would scream out in her sleep, *"Nicht schlagen!"* ("Don't beat me!")

As the Allied forces advanced, the Germans started the evacuation of prisoners so there would be no eyewitnesses to tell what had happened. If evacuation to the Tyrol Alps was not possible, mass execution was to take place through machine gun fire or bombing.

The prisoners from Geislingen were shipped to Allach, a sub-camp of Dachau, where BMW used slave labor to produce automotive parts for the Germans. When Dachau and Allach were evacuated, Helen was put onto a train of open boxcars and became one of 3000 hostages for the SS High Command. At the same time, 7000 prisoners left Dachau on a death march.

On April 29, 1945, the train was liberated by the American Army in Staltach, south of Munich, just several hours before explosive charges planted by the Germans were set to go off to blow up the train.

Once she was liberated by the American troops, Helen spent a year recuperating in a hospital. She married David's father, Vilmos, immigrated to America and settled in Brooklyn, where David and his two sisters, Sharon and Malka, were raised. Helen was successful in rebuilding a happy family life filled with love and kindness.

Events happen because they are possible. If they were possible once, they are possible again. In that sense the Holocaust is not unique, but a warning for the future.

Yehuda Bauer
"Is the Holocaust Unique?"
Perspectives on Comparative Genocide in The Holocaust in Historical Perspective, 1978

EPILOGUE

GENOCIDE

Since the beginning of the 20th century more than 50 million individuals have been murdered in acts of genocide and ethnic cleansing. It is the equivalent of wiping out the entire populations of Hungary, Portugal, Sweden, Switzerland, Greece, Finland, Puerto Rico, and Denmark. When you think about these deaths as disappearing populations, you can begin to understand the enormity of this number.

Each of these 50 million individuals was a son, a daughter, a sister, a brother, a father, a mother, an aunt, an uncle, a cousin, a loved one, a friend of someone somewhere. Each of these 50 million lives was precious. Each of these individuals had the potential to bring something new and special into the world.

We cannot fathom what talents and new universes were destroyed. We can only memorialize those who died and speak out on their behalf so that genocides do not continue to happen.

The term "genocide" was coined in 1944 by Raphael Lemkin, a Polish-Jewish legal scholar, from *geno-* the Greek word for family, tribe or race, and *–cide*, the Latin word for massacre, to describe the Holocaust and the Armenian genocide. Lemkin escaped the Holocaust by fleeing Warsaw for Sweden in 1940, coming to the United States in 1941.

The international legal definition of *genocide* consists of two main elements: the mental element—the "intent" to destroy, in whole or in part, a national, ethnic, racial or religious group—and the physical act—that meets five criteria:

1. Killing members of the group.
2. Causing serious bodily or mental harm to members of the group.
3. Deliberately inflicting conditions of life calculated to bring about the group's physical destruction, in whole or in part.
4. Imposing measures intended to prevent births within the group.
5. Forcibly transferring children of the group to another group.

"Ethnic cleansing" refers to practices aimed at the displacement or murder of an ethnic group from a particular territory to create "ethnically pure" societies. This is what happened in the Balkans and Sudan at the turn of the 21st century. In the Balkans, in the 1990s, Christians attacked Muslims. It is estimated that 250,000 Muslims were killed in those wars. In 2008, in Sudan, Arab Muslims displaced black African Muslims in Darfur, their southern province. So far more than 500 villages have been destroyed and 2,000,000 people have been dispossessed; as many as 500,000 men, women and children have been killed.

In the last century, millions upon millions of additional people have been killed by their own leaders: Stalin of Russia from the 1930-50s (estimates range from 20-30 million), Mao Zedong of China, from the 1950s-70s (estimates range from 40-78 million); and Pol Pot during the '70s killed some 2 million people in Cambodia. While not officially declared genocide, these deaths were, in fact, genocide.

The murders of 50 million men, women, and children took place in civilized nations in the West (during the Holocaust, Bosnia, Kosovo) as well as in tribal societies around the world (Rwanda, Sudan, Burundi, Biafra). They continue to take place. Astonishingly, many of these acts occur under "the rule of law," with the encouragement and imprimatur of governments and their citizens.

GENOCIDES SINCE 1915

NATION	YEAR	TARGET
Ottoman Empire	1915	Armenians
Soviet Union	1932	Ukrainians
The Holocaust	1935-45	Jews: also Gypsies [Roma and Sinti] Jehovah's Witnesses, German & Austrian male homosexuals*, disabled people political dissidents
Biafra	1966	Biafrans by Nigerians
Paraguay	1968	Ache Indians
Bangladesh	1971	Hindus
Burundi	1972	Hutus
Cambodia	1975	Non-communists, religious people minority ethnic groups
Guatemala	1982	Mayan Indians
Iraq	1988	Kurds
Somalia	1991	Bantus
Rwanda	1993	Tutsis
Bosnia	1995	Muslims
Kosovo	1998	Muslims
East Timor	1999	Catholics
Sudan	continues	Darfur
Tibet	continues	Buddhists

*"The only case of killing of gay people occurred under the Nazis, but it was limited to around 1,000 individuals, maybe slightly more, out of the 1.5 to 3 million homosexuals in pre-Hitler Germany. This is hardly a genocide, though, of course, it is bad enough in itself." —Yehuda Bauer.

The missionaries of Christianity had said in effect: You have no right to live among us as Jews. The secular rulers who followed had proclaimed: You have no right to live among us. The German Nazis at last decried, "You have no right to live."

Raul Hilberg
The Destruction of European Jewry

A CONCISE HISTORY OF
THE HOLOCAUST

ॐॐ

During the Holocaust, millions of Jewish people were murdered by the Germans and their collaborators because they were Jews.

The Jews were an easy target for almost 2,000 years, from 70 C.E., when the Jews were exiled from their homeland, until after World War II. For centuries, the Catholic Church — which became the Holy Roman Empire in the Middle Ages — ruled most of Europe and taught that Christianity's truth was Judaism's error; that the Jews had been given the divine revelation and misunderstood it. They accused the Jews of killing Jesus and claimed that all Jews were culpable for eternity unless they converted.

Set apart from society, Jews who refused to convert were treated with contempt and were murdered by mobs incited to violence by Christian clergy and local rulers. In many countries, the Jews were forced to live in closed-off areas called ghettos. By the Middle Ages, the Jews were despised by Catholics, Protestants, and Muslims. In some places, they were barred from owning property; could not join guilds (trade unions), and were solely allowed to be money lenders, and used as tax collectors and pawnbrokers — professions that only increased the enmity against them. In the 9th century, the Muslims, who treated Christians and Jews as second-class citizens, forced their Jews to wear yellow badges, and later, the Catholics, under Pope Innocent III, at the turn of the 13th century, did the same.[1]

This prejudice and hostility toward Jews is called antisemitism. Based on religious/political differences with roots in religious superiority, it was sometimes lethal and ebbed and flowed throughout the centuries. Usually, the only way for a Jew to avoid persecution was to convert to Christianity in Christian countries, or to Islam in Islamic countries. By the 20th century, though Christian churches had lost much of their political power, religious/political antisemitism continued to exist. New racial theories transformed it into race hatred of the Jews that sometimes manifested itself in bizzare accusations.

Jews are forbidden by biblical law to ingest any blood.[2] Yet for centuries blood libels falsely accused them of murdering Christian children and using their blood in matzos, the flatbread they eat during the week of Passover. (The holiday commemorates the Israelite exodus from Egypt and their liberation from slavery.) This accusation is called a blood libel.

During the 12th and 13th centuries, there were at least a dozen blood libels in Europe that caused thousands of Jews to be slaughtered and burned alive in England, France, Germany, Italy, Spain, and Austria. This same lie was used by Hitler to spread antisemtism and is being spread today, with some variations, by antisemites and radical Islamic media throughout the world.

WHY DOES HISTORY MATTER?

History matters because it shows us how genocide happens and alerts us to the methods that lead to the madness.

After Adolf Hitler came to power in Germany in 1933, his National Socialist Party (the Nazis) adapted many historical and church practices to facilitate their secular racism. These practices included blood libels against the Jews, making Jews wear yellow badges (the Yellow Star), taking away their jobs, confiscating their homes, looting their assets and forcing Jews into ghettos. The antisemites also destroyed synagogues and Jewish places of learning, and ultimately murdered the Jews themselves. Throughout the Middle Ages in Europe this was usual, although there were periods of calm. Hitler modernized these techniques and exploited this kind of antisemitism in the 20th century.

EXPULSION & EXPANSION

Throughout the Middle Ages, from the 5th to 16th centuries, Jews were expelled from many European countries and their assets looted. Historian Ellis Rivkin says that the fate of the Jews always hinged on economic policies. He describes how through the centuries, whenever there was economic expansion in a given region, life was basically good for the Jews. But when the economy contracted, the Jews often became the victims of the surrounding society's financial frustrations and targets for its violence. They lived at the whim of local populations and authorities, and were often forced to leave, while their posessions remained behind.[3]

In the 15th century, Jewish victimization was most prevalent in Spain, a country where Jews had prospered and lived in peace for 500 years. By 1391, because of the fervent practice of Catholicism, thousands of Jews were tortured, killed or forced into baptism. Because of that, a new class of Jewish Christians emerged, the *Conversos*. Many of these converted Jews were tortured during the Inquisition to force them to admit their conversions were false and that they remained "secret Jews." Thousands were murdered and their property confiscated. In 1492, all non-converted Jews had their possessions confiscated and were banished from Spain. Portugal did the same to its Jews in 1497.

As a result, tens of thousands of Jews moved to Islamic countries, the Ottoman Empire, Poland-Lithuania, Russia and Holland. There they were welcomed by governments that sought economic growth. By the 20th century, the Jewish population that fled to Central and Eastern Europe 500 years earlier had grown to more than 9,000,000.

THE BIG LIE

In 1881, in Russia, Jews were falsely accused of assassinating Czar Alexander II. As a consequence, they became victims of government-sanctioned pogroms (mob riots). Then, in 1905, the Russian Czarist antisemitic fabrication, *The Protocols of the Elders of Zion*, was published. It declared that the Jews were secretly conspiring to rule the world. Though proven to be a hoax, its lies were spread everywhere. The book—in the 21st century—is a bestseller in Islamic countries.

MODERNIZATION & MAYHEM

By the 19th century, the Roman Catholic Church lost its almost universal power in Europe as a result of the Enlightenment. Monarchies were overthrown, colonial empires collapsed, and agrarian societies were industrialized. Reason and science were supposed to supplant the superstitions of religion. But this didn't really alter attitudes and conditions for the Jews, who, despite some attempts to assimilate, were still despised. Though secular intellectuals and philosophers disdained organized Christianity, they blamed its creation on the Jews and held them collectively guilty for Christianity's brutality through the ages.

The development of modernity—science, psychology, nationalism, and the Industrial Age—caused huge economic and social turmoil. One response to this chaos was Adolf Hitler's creation of the National Socialist Party (Nazis) in Germany in 1919. A rabid antisemite, Hitler married his party to fervent nationalism and the new racial theories of eugenics: the study of hereditary improvement of the human race by controlled selective breeding. This new racial science became central to Nazi ideology and was combined with its ambition to conquer land and natural resources from other nations to create the Thousand-Year Reich — the Nazi plan to rule the world.

It was no accident, then, that when the modern era began, the rationale and technology for killing Jews was also modernized. Hitler and the Nazis used psychology to dehumanize the Jews; mass media to spread their new brand of antisemitism, and new industrial techniques to carry out their murder.

HOW DID HITLER COME TO POWER?

After her defeat in 1917, Germany was punished for starting World War I by being forced to sign the Treaty of Versailles. As a result, Germany lost its colonies in Africa and territory it had previously conquered — including parts of France, Belgium, Poland, and Czechoslovakia. Germany was forbidden to manufacture, export and/or import arms and tanks, to have poison gas, or an army beyond 100,000 men. Its navy was limited to 15,000 men.

Once the treaty was signed, the Germans felt powerless. German markets shrank and, in the early 1920s, Germany's currency collapsed so drastically that prices of even the most basic staples would increase geometrically overnight. A loaf of bread cost a wheelbarrow full of Deutsche Marks.

Stumping for the Nazi Party, Hitler was the first politician in Germany to use modern campaign techniques: radio and film, as well as print to bring his message to the people. He crisscrossed Germany by plane, made speeches everywhere, and played to the German citizens' sense of shame and loss by blaming Jewish bankers for the Treaty of Versailles. He encouraged Germans to focus on nationalism, ethnic and racial identity, geographic and economic expansion, and military might.

While many Germans may have disagreed with the Nazis'

virulent antisemitic policies, what was more important to them was their fervent nationalism and economic reconstruction. As a result, Hitler met with little resistance. For a long time, Germans also did not take Nazi Party violence seriously. But by 1922, before Hitler's [1923] Beer Hall *Putsch* (an attempt by Hitler and his followers to overthrow the German government), his followers had already murdered 344 opponents. Still, even the *New York Times*, at that time, referred to the Nazis as "a bunch of unruly Boy Scouts."[4]

BIG BUSINESS

By 1932, Germany's big businesses and middle class were worried that the combination of economic dislocation and political chaos would destroy the Weimar Republic, the German democratic government that had replaced the German monarchy. Germany's businessmen supported Hitler because they saw opportunities for economic gain and thought they would be able to influence his policies. Established politicians, recognizing how popular Nazi ideas were, felt that by bringing Hitler into the upper reaches of the government they could control him and gain the upper hand. The businessmen and politicians were both wrong.

On January 30, 1933, the President of Germany, Paul von Hindenberg, seeking political stability for the Weimar Republic, appointed Hitler head of the coalition government. Less than a month later, the Reichstag, the German parliament building, was set ablaze. A Dutch communist was blamed, but it was believed that the Nazis had done it. The next day, Hitler had von Hindenberg sign the Emergency Decree "for the Protection of the people and the State." This allowed the government to restrict personal liberty, freedom of expression, and freedom of the press. The decree limited the right of assembly and association and allowed violations of privacy in postal, telegraphic and telephone communications. The government could issue warrants for house searches, confiscations and restrictions on property "beyond the legal limits otherwise prescribed."

Three weeks later, on March 23, Hitler passed the "Enabling Act," giving him control of the constitutional functions of the government. Within days, Nazi paramilitary troops took over local state governments and arrested and imprisoned thousands of the Nazi Party's political opponents.

Piece by piece, Hitler began to slowly break the Treaty of Versailles. He reconstituted the German army and used the latest weapons, automotive and aeronautic technologies to rearm and rebuild the country's military might.

Just 51 days after coming into office, Hitler opened Dachau, a concentration camp for his political opponents. Thousands of communists and vocal critics of the regime were arrested and imprisoned there. Though only a small number of the prisoners at that time were Jews, the camp became a model for all the subsequent concentration and death camps used to contain, enslave, and murder Jews and others deemed expendable by the state.

OUT OF THE BLUE

Though most Jews could never be part of the fabric of European life, after the Enlightenment many held high positions in government, the military, academia and the civil service. For instance, there were more than 500,000 Jews living in Germany between the wars. More than 100,000 of them—one in six—served in World War I; 12,000 died in combat.[5] In Poland, Hungary ,and other Central and Eastern European countries, Jews were also complacent and did not realize that the terror being hatched in Germany by the Nazis would soon envelop them as well.

Until the Nazis put their policies into effect, antisemitism was escapable by converting to Christianity. When the racial theorists and Nazis created their brand of antisemitism, they separated the Jews from the rest of the population. Under Nazi rule, there was no way to escape one's Jewishness.

THE WAR AGAINST THE JEWS

The war against the Jews began on April 1, 1933, when the Nazis called for a boycott of Jewish businesses. All Jewish civil servants, including doctors and lawyers, were soon fired. A quota system limiting Jewish access to schools, universities, trades and professions was established.[6] In May, in 30 cities, German students and their professors burned hundreds of thousands of books, the majority of them by Jewish authors.[7]

Heinrich Heine, a German poet of Jewish origin who lived a century earlier, once said, "Where one burns books, one will, in the end, burn people."[8] Historian Michael Berenbaum notes that in Nazi Germany it took eight years from the time Jewish books were burned to the burning of the Jews themselves.[9]

THE GERMANS BEGIN BY KILLING THEIR OWN

Because the Nazis sought genetic superiority for their master race, when he became the German leader Hitler began a program that, at first, sterilized mentally and physically disabled adults. He also ordered German doctors to kill German infants and children who were mentally and physically challenged.[10] They did as he asked. By October 1939, under T4 — the forced euthanasia program — the Nazis moved from sterilizing to murdering disabled teenagers and adults. They installed gas chambers at six killing centers. Carbon monoxide was released into sealed rooms disguised as showers, where many disabled people were murdered at once. Large crematoria were built to dispose of the bodies. The ashes of the dead were sent to their families, who were told their relatives had died of natural causes or disease.

When the German people discovered the T4 program, they demanded it be stopped. Although the gassing stopped on German soil, the killing continued with pre-gassing methods.

Instead, the Nazis used the T4 killing centers to murder concentration camp prisoners. After the expansion of killing centers at Auschwitz-Birkenau in 1943, the T4 killing centers were no longer needed.[11]

THE NUREMBERG LAWS

In 1935 the Nazis passed the Nuremberg Laws for the "Protection of German Blood and German Honor and the Law of the Reich Citizen." These laws restricted Jewish life even more and became the guide for defining and categorizing Jews in all future German-occupied countries. The creation of these categories was the beginning of the dehumanization process. The Germans legalized racial (as well as religious) antisemitism, placing Jews outside of the protection of the State and setting the stage for their destruction.[12] (*See Appendix One, The Nuremberg Laws.*)

Though the Nazis were recalcitrant racists and murderers, they were sensitive to international public opinion. In 1931, Germany won the right to host the Summer Olympics in 1936. Hitler regarded the games as essential to international acceptance of the Nazi domination of Germany and used public relations techniques to keep criticism down. During the games, antisemitic signs normally posted around Berlin were removed and German newspapers toned down their rhetoric. International visitors saw a Germany that was more benign than it actually was. But by participating in the games instead of boycotting them, the free nations of the world reinforced Hitler's belief that they agreed with his anti-Jewish policies. Once the games were over, the Nazis stepped up their persecution.[13]

THE EVIAN CONFERENCE

As German anti-Jewish policies continued to expand, German Jews realized that life was no longer viable in Germany. Though they wanted to leave, many could not do so—especially the poor—because they discovered that no country would have them, and those that would required financial guarantees so that refugees would not become wards of the State.[14]

U.S. President Franklin D. Roosevelt convened a conference in Evian, a resort town in France, in July 1938 to discuss the problem of refugees. In those days, "refugees" was a euphemism for Jews. For nine days 32 countries debated the fate of Jewish refugees and decided they couldn't accept them because of indigenous antisemitism and unstable economic conditions in their own countries. Only the Dominican Republic, an island country in the Caribbean, was willing to accept Jews—for a price. In short, there was no place for Jews anywhere.

Following World War I, when the British took control of the former territories of the Ottoman Empire, its 1917 Balfour Declaration promised Jews a homeland in Mandate Palestine. But as Arab resistance mounted, the land mass of the designated Jewish homeland was further and further diminished. Even so, on the eve of World War II, 400,000 Jews lived there. As the pressure on Jews in Germany intensified, and with the lack of open doors around the world through which to flee, Jews looked to Palestine as a potential port in the approaching storm.

But Britain put the brakes on this hoped for escape. To appease the demands of Arab rulers in the Middle East who controlled the oil that fueled England's airplanes, tanks and ships, in May 1939 the British slammed the door on Jewish immigration. They issued the McDonald White Paper limiting Jewish immigration to 15,000 Jews a year—at a time when millions of Jews were attempting to escape from Europe. During the Parliamentary debate, Lloyd George described the White Paper as "an act of perfidy" and Winston Churchill, then a member of Parliament, voted against it. The *Manchester Guardian* described the document as "a death sentence on tens of thousands of Central European Jews."[15] However, the British did bring 10,000 Jewish children to England during the war (the *Kindertransportees*). Most of these children's parents were killed during the Holocaust.

KRISTALLNACHT: NIGHT OF BROKEN GLASS

In March 1938 Hitler annexed Austria (the *Anschluss*). Then, in October, he moved his troops into resource-rich Czechoslovakia. Although there were alliances, the major powers, Britain and France, allowed him to do so for the sake of peace. Decried as appeasment, their hoped-for peace machinations nevertheless failed.

During the late night and early morning hours of November 9-10, 1938, in Germany and Austria, there were nationwide government coordinated acts of terrorism against the Jews. Conceived by Minister of Propaganda Joseph Goebbels, and ordered by the Gestapo (the Nazi secret police headed by Hermann Goering), Nazi Party paramilitary troops (the Brownshirts/S.A.), destroyed and looted more than 1,400 synagogues and 7,500 Jewish businesses; 91 Jews were murdered, and 30,000 Jewish men ages 16-60 were arrested and/or tortured.[16] The broken glass from the synagogues and shop windows gave the pogrom its name, *Kristallnacht*. Today, that night is considered the opening chapter of the Holocaust.

Regular police and other authorities stood idly by as shops and homes were burglarized and looted. Firefighters watched as synagogues burned. Their only instructions were to ensure that nearby homes or buildings did not catch fire. The response in the United States was blistering, though many Protestant and Catholic Church leaders in Germany applauded the desecration and destruction of the synagogues.

According to the Nazis, the violence of *Kristallnacht* was triggered by Herschel Grynszpan, a distraught 17-year-old who had assassinated Ernst von Rath, a German Embassy official in Paris. The boy was furious at the way the Germans had treated his parents, who were dumped and left to starve with thousands of other non-German Jews on the Polish border. Grynzspan was held for 20 months by the French. In June 1940, when the French capitulated to the Germans, the

French government handed him over to the Gestapo in Berlin, whereupon he disappeared.[17]

To add insult to injury, though the violence of *Kristallnacht* should have been covered by insurance, Jews were forbidden to file claims against German insurance companies. But non-Jewish landlords owned some of the shops that had broken windows, and non-Jewish companies lost 20 to 30 percent of their exports. Because *Kristallnacht* proved so costly to the Germans, there were no more public riots. In addition, the German Jewish community was forced to pay a one billion Deutsche Mark fine, as well as fines for Grynszpan's assassination of von Rath and the clean-up costs from *Kristallnacht*.

Almost immediately the noose around German Jews tightened even more. They were barred from schools, banned from public places, and their businesses were forcibly sold to non-Jews. It became clear to German Jews that normal community life was no longer possible in Germany. Many tried to flee; some committed suicide. By the time World War II began, about half of the German Jewish population (250,000) and one-third of the Austrian Jewish population fled, many to neighboring countries — only to be trapped again later, during the German conquest of Europe.

THE WORLD WAR BEGINS

Hitler, in a secret agreement with the Soviet Union, attacked Poland on September 1, 1939. With the invasion, millions of Polish Jews in western Poland fell under German rule and millions more were subjected to the control of the Soviets in the East. France and Belgium quickly fell in June 1940. Vichy France, a puppet French government, aligned itself with the Germans. In September 1940, Italy and Japan officially became Germany's allies. Then, in June 1941, Germany reneged on its agreements with Russia and attacked its former partner. As the troops headed East, the Germans also began systematically executing Jews *en masse*.

When the Germans originally began to discriminate against the Jews, the plan was to force them to emigrate. But when the Germans conquered most of Europe, they took control of more Jews than they could handle. And when it became clear no other country would take their new charges, the Nazis considered literally shipping all of them to Madagascar. However, the expense made the idea impractical. Although the Nazis had stripped the Jews of all their assets, the costs involved in transporting them to Madagascar were beyond consideration.

As a result of the Polish conquest and the expansion eastward, by 1942, the Nazis had 11 million Jews under their control, including those in Western Europe. What were they going to do with them? Hitler had promised to rid Europe of its Jews, but where would he send them?

JUDENRÄTE & GHETTOIZATION

The Nazis needed to quickly do something. First, they established Jewish Councils, *Judenräte*, deluding Jewish community leaders into helping them carry out their anti-Jewish policies in their local communities.

Often the Germans appointed people at random because the first and second groups of appointed council members would resign or refused to agree to German demands. Those people were usually deported or murdered. As such, Jewish communities acted no differently than other populations under Nazi-ruled Europe. In countries that came under German occupation, local administrations were set up. Almost all of the conquered country community leaders, mayors and police chiefs followed the directives and orders of the Germans. How many opposed the Germans? Hardly any.

Once they established formalized operational agencies, the Germans recruited local collaborators to help them round up Jews and put them into overcrowded ghettos—small enclosed areas in cities and towns that separated the Jews from the rest of society. In the Warsaw Ghetto, for example, nine people, on average, were forced to live in one room.

Slowly, the Nazis and their collaborators began to choke off food supplies, water, and medicine to the ghettos, systematically starving the residents and creating conditions rife for typhus and tuberculosis epidemics. These further decimated ghetto populations. By war's end, there were more than 1,000 ghettos and thousands of camps in German-occupied Europe that had imprisoned millions of victims, Jews and non-Jews.[18]

EINSATZGRUPPEN

As the German army marched through Poland and into Lithuania, and Russia, it was followed by special killing and looting squads called *Einsatzgruppen*. These squads dragged Jews from their homes and forced them to dig their own mass graves. Then these squads shot them and buried them on the spot. In Babi Yar, outside Kiev in Ukraine, these battalions slaughtered more than 33,000 Jews.[19]

But *Einsatzgruppen* were not cost effective enough for the Nazi accountants because they could not murder Jews fast enough—and bullets were expensive. In addition, the killings were a psychological burden on the shooters. Despite these "problems," it is estimated that *Einsatzgruppen* killed over 1,000,000 people, more than 90 percent of them Jews.

Soon, however, the Germans determined it would be more efficient to bring victims to central killing places, and the newest tool in the Nazi arsenal became the death camps. In those death factories, gas chambers modeled after the euthanasia killing centers of the T4 program were set up and systematic, assembly-line techniques were instituted for committing mass murder.

THE WANNSEE CONFERENCE

The Wannsee Conference was held on January 20, 1942. Its aim was to create a smoothly operating bureaucratic and logistics machine to supply the killing factories with their human "fodder" as impersonally and cost-effectively as possible.

Those who attended the meeting were some of Germany's best and brightest—the ranking "number two" officials—men in major government departments and the party apparatus who knew how to cut red tape. Most were young lawyers; eight had doctorates.[20]

Europe was to be combed for Jews to be removed to the East, where most of the slave labor and death camps were built. In order to prevent panic, the psychologists determined it would make sense to have people send postcards to those left behind to make them believe all was relatively well. But relocating millions of people to the East was a logistical nightmare, even if they could be hidden in the mass movements of war refugees. The chief coordinator of this enormous enterprise would be Heinrich Himmler, head of the SS (the *Schutzstaffel*, Nazi Storm Troopers), who oversaw all police and security forces, including the Gestapo (the political police force of the Reich) and *Einsatzgruppen*. Adolf Eichmann was his right-hand man.

Once the meeting was over, key agencies and their leadership were informed of the decisions and were told the SS was in charge. The heads of the agencies capitulated to that arrangement.

THE RAPE OF A PEOPLE

German soldiers who invaded towns, cities or villages sent home millions of packages containing jewelry, clothing, false teeth, works of art, stamp collections, pottery, furniture, glassware, and even food. Many local non-Jews and collaborators also took over Jewish homes and possessions, enriching themselves.

Major corporations paid the Nazis for Jewish slave labor.

Fed less than subsistence rations and housed in horrendous conditions with no sanitary facilities, the Jews were literally worked to death.

The Germans wasted nothing. When the death camps were first opened, the victims' hair was turned into wigs and blankets, and the gold extracted from their teeth was used, in part, to pay for Germany's war.

INDUSTRIALIZING MASS MURDER

The gas chambers from the T4 forced euthanasia program were prototypes for the Nazi death camps at Belzec, Sobibor, Treblinka, Majdanek, Chelmno, and Auschwitz — all of them in German-occupied Poland.

Auschwitz, the largest death camp, was founded in 1940 to hold political and criminal prisoners. It was expanded in 1942 into an efficient death factory modeled on industrial principles. Living conditions were deplorable, infinitely worse than those in the ghettos. Sanitary conditions didn't exist. Camp hospitals were used for human medical experiments.

Auschwitz sat on approximately 25 square miles and by the end of the war had three main camps: Auschwitz I, the receiving/holding camp; Auschwitz-Birkenau, the giant killing center, and Auschwitz Monowitz, where the I.G. Farben rubber factory was located. The killing center, Birkenau, was 1.5 miles long, a mile wide and held 200,000 people in more than 300 buildings. At first, almost 4,500 people a day were murdered there. Later, efficiency experts almost doubled the killing rate to 8,000 a day. More than 90 percent of those who were murdered in Birkenau between 1942 and 1945 were Jews.[21]

By the time they occupied Hungary in March 1944, the Nazi process was refined to a science. They were able to round up and deport 437,402 Hungarian Jews to Auschwitz in just three months.

In March, 1942, before the implementation of the Wannsee "Final Solution" policies, 75 to 80 percent of the Jews in Europe were alive. Eleven months later, 75 to 80 percent of the Jews in Europe were dead.[22]

ISOLATION, ABANDONMENT AND A GLIMMER OF HOPE

The Germans had designed a social system that effectively turned their citizens and those under their occupation into bystanders or collaborators. Most people living near the death and slave labor camps could see the conditions and smell the smoke from the crematoria but pretended they didn't know what was happening.

Even so, there were flickers of hope. Among the hundreds of millions of non-Jews in Europe, tens of thousands attempted to help Jews while risking their own lives. Today, the Avenue of the Righteous at Yad Vashem, Israel's Holocaust Authority and educational center, has planted thousands of trees in their honor. Sometimes individuals saved many, sometimes many saved an individual. So far, some 22,000 non-Jews from 44 countries have been remembered for risking their lives to save Jews.[23]

For the most part, the victims of the Nazi regime were turned into a despairing mass, too weak spiritually or physically to defy their torturers. And yet, despite all odds, there were those who defied Nazi attempts to strip them of their dignity and hope. There were pockets of successful physical resistance in the ghettos, in the forests and even in the concentration and death camps. (*See Chapter 10,* The Bold and the Brave.)

THE AMERICAN REACTION

Before the war, Americans were isolationists who wanted to stay away from European entanglements. When it concerned the persecution of the Jews in Germany, they didn't want to get involved in what they felt were Germany's internal policies. Also, because the unemployment rate in America was at 25 percent, the American people were overwhelmingly opposed to allowing new immigrants in. President Roosevelt was not about to challenge them.

It did not help that antisemitism was a functioning component of the American social landscape. Just one example was the popular Roman Catholic priest, Father Charles Coughlin, now considered the father of hate speech radio. Every Sunday morning after Mass, he spewed antisemitism on the national airwaves.

Adding to the problem of immigration was Breckenridge Long. An avowed antisemite, Long headed the U.S. Department of Immigration and Naturalization. He constantly argued that letting Jews into America would create a "fifth column" — a group of people who secretly undermine a larger group that expects it to be loyal. Long also said Jews from Poland and Russia "are lawless, scheming, defiant...just the same as the criminal Jews who crowd our police court dockets in New York."[24]

Though there were bureaucrats like Long at the State Department, there were others who did care. In 1944, John Pehle, Randolph Paul, and Josaiah DuBois prepared the "Personal Report to the President" about what was happening to the Jews in Europe. They threatened to resign if Treasury Secretary Henry Morgenthau didn't send it to the President. Morgenthau sent it and the memo led to Roosevelt's creation of the War Refugee Board (WRB).

Raoul Wallenberg, a young Swedish diplomat, was a member of the WRB and the most effective rescuer of Jews. He went to Budapest and provided safe houses, effectively stopping the deportations of 230,000 people. As the war ended in 1945, the Soviets entered the city,

*(You can learn about Wallenberg at http://www.ushmm.org/wlc/article.php?ModuleId=10005211)

whereupon Wallenberg disappeared into the Soviet prison system and was never seen or heard from again. Though governments around the world have asked for information, the Soviets continue to stonewall, saying nothing.*

The WRB also organized the transfer of 48,000 Jews from Transnistria in southeastern Europe to safe areas in Romania, and allowed 982 Jews into Oswego, New York, where they were interned behind barbed-wire fences from 1944 to 1946.

The American Jewish community itself was divided on what it should do to help the Jews trapped in Europe. Some Jewish leaders wanted to keep a low profile in order not to confront the rampant antisemitism in America. Others felt that they had to protest publicly to demand a change in policy so that the Jews of Europe could be rescued. Still others felt that the American Jewish community priority should be to push for the creation of the State of Israel. They felt that instead of concentrating on rescue, they needed a homeland so that Jews would have somewhere to go.

THE HOLOCAUST WENT BEYOND EUROPE

The Holocaust took place in what are now 35 countries around the world and affected each one of them differently. In many of these countries, the locals were more than happy to collaborate in the destruction of their Jewish neighbors. France, Hungary, Poland, Romania, and Croatia were overly adept at ridding themselves of their Jewish population. Only Denmark made a concerted effort to save its Jews. Bulgaria, on the other hand, saved its own Jews but deported the Jews from Macedonia, Croatia, and Thrace in the Balkans.

Europe was not the only region to be "cleansed" of its Jews. As German troops moved toward Palestine from North Africa and across the Mediterranean from Cyprus, Greece, and Rhodes, Jews were separated and segregated from local populations and either killed on the spot or deported to death and labor camps in Eastern Europe.

Ironically, although they were allied with Germany, the Japanese created a Jewish quarter in Shanghai, their colony in China. Mostly German Jewish refugees and other Jews who had escaped through Kobe, Japan, lived there. It was a difficult life and many people starved, but when the Nazis decided they wanted to deport those Jews, the Japanese refused to let them go.

When France fell in 1940, Syria and Lebanon (French colonies in the Middle East) came under the control of the Vichy government. As such, the 30,000 Jews in Syria became victims of the Nuremberg Laws. Jewish businesses were confiscated and Jews were interned in detention camps. Fortunately, the British and Free French forces seized control before Henri Dentz, the Syrian high commissioner, could open concentration camps. On July 15, 1940, German allies bombed Haifa and Tel Aviv, injuring hundreds.

In May 1941 the Grand Mufti of Jerusalem, Mohammad Amin al-Husayni, leader of the Arabs in British Mandate Palestine, met with Hitler in Berlin. Rabidly antisemitic, he said he would be happy to help Hitler deal with the Jews in Palestine.

In 1942, one of Germany's greatest generals, Erwin Rommel, crossed Egypt to El Alamein, threatening Mandate Palestine. The 400,000 Jews who lived there were terrified that the British would abandon them to the Germans and the Grand Mufti. It took until October 1943 for British General Bernard Montgomery to stop Rommel's army and end the German threat. That same month, the Russian victory at Stalingrad marked the beginning of the fall of Nazi Germany.

BLACKS DURING THE HOLOCAUST

Historian Robert Kesting estimates that there were 1,000 to 1,500 Blacks in Germany between 1933 and 1936. Since the Black population was miniscule, there was no systematic plan to annihilate them as there was for Jews.[25] Nevertheless, in 1937, the Gestapo rounded up all the Blacks it could find. They sterilized them, used them for medical experiments, or "disappeared" them. Black musicians, artists, and dancers under German occupation were sent to the Falkensee concentration camp in Czechoslovakia.[26]

Some Black Americans, caught in German-occupied Europe during World War II, also became victims of the Nazis. Western European, British, and American Blacks were deported to concentration camps — Mauthausen, Buchenwald, Dora-Mittelbau, Dachau, and Sachsenhausen. They were kept in segregated barracks and were worked to death alongside the Jews.

WAR'S END

From the beginning, the Jews prayed for the Allies, especially the Americans, to rescue them. But the United States did not officially join France and England in World War II until it was attacked by the Japanese at Pearl Harbor on December 7, 1941. Four days later, Germany declared war on the United States.

Even so, before D-Day, June 6, 1944, the day the Allied troops landed on the beaches of Normandy, France, most of America's battles were fought in the Pacific theater against the Japanese, not in Europe.

After the Allies invaded Europe and it became obvious the Germans would lose the war, the Nazis still continued to divert badly needed resources to their first priority: killing the Jews of Europe. When the Allies finally liberated the camps, beginning in the summer of 1944, they discovered that approximately 6,000,000 Jews, two-thirds of the Jewish people in Europe, had lived and died under indescribably inhumane conditions.[27]

Of all the people murdered in the death camps, 90 percent were Jews. In *Aktion Reinhard*, the plan to murder the Jews of German-occupied Poland in such death camps as Belzec, Sobibor, and Treblinka, 99.99 percent of the victims were Jews.

The Nazis also murdered a minimum of 90,000 to 200,000 Sinti and Roma, although the precise number cannot be determined. Hundreds of thousands of others were also killed: the physically and mentally disabled, male homosexuals, Jehovah's Witnesses, socialists, communists, trade unionists, and political and religious dissidents.[28] All told, during World War II, approximately 59 million people, including soldiers, died.

When World War II and the Holocaust finally ended, there were many in the German military hierarchy and those in the general German population who claimed they did not know what the Nazis and their collaborators had done to the Jews. This was a lie. 64,427 tapes of conversations from 10,191 German prisoners, including senior officers, were recorded by the British Secret Intelligence Service from 1942 to 1945. They clearly describe the slaughter of the Jews and German participation in it.[29]

LAND OF THE FREE AND HOME OF THE BRAVE

Throughout the war, the victims caught in the Holocaust prayed for liberation by the American troops. Ignorant of the political and military limitations of American power, America, nonetheless, was to them the *"Goldeneh Medina,"* the land where dreams come true. Despite its foibles and weaknesses, they believed that in America they could be free to practice their Judaism or be free from religion altogether, and that no one would care. They knew that they could rebuild their lives in a land of democracy and meritocracy, where if they worked hard they could be successful.

VATICAN II, AN ACT OF CONTRITION

In 1965, the Roman Catholic Church issued *Nostra Aetate*, a document from the Second Vatican Council. It made many changes in Catholic doctrine and repudiated the notion that the Jews were collectively and eternally guilty of deicide.

Jews have lived in Rome since the days of St. Peter in the first century C.E. St. Peter served as the first Bishop of Rome, as do all Popes. Yet it took nearly 2,000 years of intermittent persecution and the Holocaust before a Pope—the Bishop of Rome— would visit a synagogue.

Pope John Paul II had been a Polish priest who witnessed the Holocaust firsthand. As a gesture of repentance for the treatment of Jews by the Church, he made the first ever visit by a Pope to Rome's Central Synagogue. While he was there, he called Jews "our beloved brothers." He expressed his abhorrence for the genocide of the Jewish people during World War II and decried antisemitic church policies that had been the norm for almost two millennia. In 2000, he journeyed to Jerusalem and asked for forgiveness for "the behavior of those who in the course of history have caused these children of yours to suffer."[30]

These acts of Catholic contrition were a direct result of the Holocaust.

NOTES

CHAPTER ONE: SILENCE = DEATH

1. "Queens Woman Is Stabbed to Death in Front of Home," *New York Times*, March 14, 1964, p. 26.

2. Nathan Stoltzfus, *Resistance of the Heart: Intermarriage and the Rosenstrasse Protest in Nazi Germany* (New Jersey: Rutgers University Press, 2001).

3. Grigoris Balakian, *Armenian Golgotha: A Memoir of the Armenian Genocide, 1915-1918* (New York: Knopf, 2009), xvii.

CHAPTER TWO: THE SNAKE MADE ME DO IT

1. http://www.dailymail.co.uk/femail/article-469883/ The-Genocide-Generals-secret-recordings-explode-myth-knew-Holocaust.html

2. *The Westminster Study Bible*, Revised Standard Version, Collins (New York: Clear Type Press, 1952), Genesis 3:1.

3. *Ibid.*, Genesis 3:11.

4. *National Geographic*, The Genographic Project, http:// genographic.nationalgeographic.com/genographic/index. html

CHAPTER THREE: CHOICES, CHOICES, CHOICES

1. Daniel Jonah Goldhagen, *Hitler's Willing Executioners: Ordinary Germans and the Holocaust* (New York: Vintage Books 1996), p. 179.
Goldhagen makes an argument using original archival material and testimony of the killers that carefully documents that the Germans had a choice to kill or not to kill Jews. The perpetrators were not coerced to kill. There is no case where a German was ever killed, sent to concentration camp,

jailed, or punished for refusing to kill Jews. In many units officers announced to their men that they did not have to kill. Himmler himself issue orders allowing those who were not up to the killing to be excused from it.

2. *Ibid.*, Goldhagen, pp. 212-222.

3. *Ibid.*, Goldhagen, p. 213. See also, Christopher R. Browning, *Ordinary Men: Reserve Police Battalion 101 and the Final Solution in Poland* (HarperCollins, 1998) p. 71. He also states that a "mere dozen men of nearly 500" asked to be excused from the massacre at Jozefow. Also p. 250, "It is also perfectly possible that one could keep away from the executions if one wanted to."

4. *Ibid.*, For further activities about Battalion 101, see Goldhagen, pp. 179-262.

5. *Ibid.*, pp. 167-168. Also see p. 537, footnote 13.
"The best source for determining the number of perpetrators is the Zentrale Stelle der Landesjustizverwaltungen zur Aufklarung nationalsozialistischet Verbrechen in Ludwigsburg (ZStL) which has been the clearing house for investigations and prosecutions of Nazi crimes since its founding in 1958. The unit catalogue (*Einheitskarten*) which contains the names of people that were suspected of being involved in an institution of killing has 333,082 cards covering 4,105 units and agencies that the authorities had a right to pursue and were involved or suspected of being involved in Nazi crimes—not only against Jews. Many of the lists are incomplete and there are many institutions that have not been investigated. The number of perpetrators was enormous; hundreds of thousands of Germans were involved in the direct murder of Jews. If we include all the persons that were involved in using slave labor, the number in the German Reich in August 1944 is over 7.6 million."

6. Stanley Milgram. *Obedience to Authority: An Experimental View* (New York: Harper & Row, 1974), p. 1ff.

7. *Ibid.*, p. 2

8. Also known as "In My Country There Is Problem," was written by the British Jewish Comedian Sacha Baron Cohen for his character Borat Sagdivev, in the 'Country Music' segment of 'Borat's Guide to the USA (Part 2)', Video clips are available on youtube.com: http://www.youtube.com/watch?v=Vb3IMTJjzfo. In interviews in the United States, Cohen said that the purpose of his film was to expose antisemitism in the United States. His gig in the Arizona Bar shows either antisemitism or indifference to antisemitism,. In an interview with *Rolling Stone* in November 14, 2006 he maintains this indifference led to the Holocaust.

9. Philip G. Zimbardo, *The Lucifer Effect: Understanding How Good People Turn Evil* (New York: Random House, 2008), p. 455.

10. Eva Fogelman, "Ideology and Individual Police Officers as Offenders, Resisters and Helpers During the Nazi Period in Germany." Speech delivered at Hochschule fur Polizei Villingen-Schwenningen.

11. Philip G. Zimbardo, "The Psychology of Power and Evil," Abstract Psychology Department, Stanford University (2005). http://www.prisonexp.org/pdf/powerevil.pdf

12. *Ethics of Our Fathers* (2:16).

CHAPTER FOUR: FREEDOM IS A PRIVILEGE

1. United States Department of State, "2008 trafficking in Persons Report" http://www.state.gov/g/tip/

2. Ann Byers, *The Trail of Tears* (New York: Rosen Publishing, 2004), p. 1ff. The author describes the removal of the Cherokee from their homes and farms in the forced march to new homes west of the Mississippi River. It claimed 4000 members of their tribe.

3. Sequoyah Research Center, April 19, 1937, Interview with

Mary Hill, Age 47, Muskogee Tribe. Ofuskee Town (tulwa) Okemah, Oklahoma. http://www.anpa.ualr.edu/digital_ library/indianvoices/family_stories/Hill.htm

4. Wayne Craig Wade, *The Fiery Cross: The Ku Klux Klan in America* (New York: Simon and Schuster, 1987), p. 273. See Norman Cohn, *Warrant For Genocide* (Hyannis, MA: Peter Myers, 2002). Although proven a blatant hoax by the Berne trial in 1935, the *Protocols* sold 120,000 copies in Germany in one year and helped convince 17 million Germans to vote for the Nazi Party in 1933. Cohn argues that this forgery helped justify the murder of two thirds of European Jewry.

5. For further information see PBS, *Children of The Camps*, http://www.pbs.org/childofcamp/

6. Nicholas Kristof, "If This Isn't Slavery, What Is?," *The New York Times*, January 4, 2009, p. 8.

7. Orson Scott Card, *Empire* (New York: Tom Doherty Associates, 2006), p. 318.

CHAPTER FIVE - JIMINY CRICKET

1. Robert S. Wistrich, *Antisemitism: The Longest Hatred* (New York: Pantheon, 1991), p. 68.

2. Michael S. Josephson and Wes Hanson, *Making Ethical Decisions* (Josephson Institute of Ethics, 1996), http://www. josephsoninstitute.org/MED/MED-5rationalizations

3. Dusan Stojanovic, "Massacre described at Kosovo war crimes trial," Fox News, December 11, 2008, http://www. foxnews.com/wires/2008Dec11/0,4670,EUSerbiaWarCrim es,00.html.

CHAPTER SIX: THE LURE OF THE DARK SIDE

1. Robert Jay Lifton, *The Nazi Doctors: Medical Killing and the Psychology of Genocide* (New York: Basic Books, 2000) p.16.

2. Yaacov Lozowick, *Hitler's Bureaucrats: The Nazi Secret Police and the Banality of Evil* (Continuum, 2005) p. 8. http://www.continuumbooks.com/Authors/detail.as px?ReturnURL=&CountryID=2&ImprintID=2&AuthorI D=144999>

3. The Nature of Power, Conflict Research Consortium, University of Colorado, USA, International Online Training Program On Intractable Conflict, http://www.colorado. edu/conflict/peace/power.htm

4. As quoted in *Spending Wisely: Buying Health Services For The Poor*, Alexander S. Preker and Jack Langenbrunner (World Bank Publications, 2005) p.285.

5. For additional discussion and background see BBC, The Hippocratic Oath. http://www.bbc.co.uk/dna/h2g2/ A1103798

6. National Public Radio, "Remembering Tuskegee, Syphilis Study Still Provokes Disbelief, Sadness," http://www.npr. org/programs/morning/features/2002/jul/tuskegee/

7. Veterans and Agent Orange: Update 2004, Institute of Medicine, of National Academy of Sciences, http://www. iom.edu/?id=28146)

CHAPTER SEVEN: WORDS CAN KILL

1. KTLA News, "Mother Convicted in Internet Suicide Case," KTLA.com, November 27, 2008. http://www.ktla.com/landing_news/?Missouri-Mom-Convicted-of-MisdemeanorCr=1&blockID=142035&feedI D=171

2. Susan Benesch, "Genocide, Pleading Free Speech," *World Policy Journal* (07-01-2004), http://ics.leeds.ac.uk/papers/ vp01.cfm?outfit=pmt&folder=193&paper=2022

3. As quoted in Sir Elihu Lauterpacht, *International Law*

*Report*s (Boston: Cambridge University Press, 1999), p. 42

4. Robert Rowen, "Gray and Black Radio Propoganda against Nazi Germany" (paper presented at the New York Military Affairs Symposium, April 18, 2003, CUNY Graduate Center) http://libraryautomation.com/nymas/radioproppaper.htm

5. Arthur G. Miller, *The Social Psychology of Good and Evil* (New York: Guilford Press, 2005), p. 498. See also, Philip G. Zimbardo, "The Psychology of Power and Evil," Abstract Psychology Department, Stanford University (2005), p. 12. http://www.prisonexp.org/pdf/powerevil.pdf

CHAPTER EIGHT: MURDER BY MUSIC

1. Donald G. McNeil JR., "Killer Songs," *New York Times*, March 17, 2002.

CHAPTER NINE: HEROES IN WAITING

1. Dwight Garner, "A War Time Tale That Had to Be Told," Books of The Times, *The New York Times*, December 26, 2008, Section C, p. 33.

2. J.K. Rowling, *Harry Potter and the Deathly Hallows* (New York: Scholastic, 2007), p. 1ff.

3. Nicholas Kristof, "Tortured, but Not Silenced," *The New York Times*, September 2, 2008. A version of this article appeared in print on August 31, 2008, on page WK11 of the New York edition.

4. Eva Fogelman, *Conscience and Courage: Rescuers of Jews During the Holocaust*, (New York: Anchor Doubleday, 1994), p. 1ff.

5. Edith Cord, *Becoming Edith* (New Milford, NJ: Wordsmithy, 2008) pp. 114-120.

6. http://www.ushmm.org/wlc/article.php?lang=en&Mo duleId=10007518mbon"

7. http://www.abadi-network.com/

8. Hadassah B. Rosensaft, *Yesterday: My Story* (Washington, D.C.: Holocaust Survivors' Memoirs Project, 2004), p. 1ff.

9. Yehudah Bauer, e-mail message to authors, September 15, 2008.

10. David Kranzler, in "Orthodox Ends, Unorthodox Means, The Role of the Hatzalah and Agudath Israel during the Holocaust," (New York: *The Goldberg Commission Report*, Maxwell Finger Editor, Appendix 4-3, City University of New York, 1985), p. 103ff.

11. Yehuda Bauer, *Jews For Sale? Nazi-Jewish negotiations, 1933-1945* (New Haven : Yale University Press,1994), p. 101.

The Europa Plan was devised by the semi-underground Jewish organization Pracovna Skupina (Working Group) in Slovakia to spare the Jews of Europe from extermination by means of ransom.

12. *Ibid.*, page 167.

13. Amos Bunim, *Irving M. Bunim, 1901-1980, The Man and His Impact on American Orthodox Jewry* (New York: Feldheim Publishers, 1989) p. 139.

14. *The Holocaust Encyclopedia*, Walter Laquer Ed., (New Haven: Yale University Press 2001) s.v. "Europa Plan" p. 165. Current scholarship shows that the bribes by Weissmandl had nothing to do with the cessation of the deportations in Slovakia.

15. *Op. cit.*, Kranzler.

16. Heather Robinson, "Roman Kent," *New York Daily News*, October 14, 2008.

17. *Ibid.*

CHAPTER TEN: THE BOLD AND THE BRAVE

1. Martin Gilbert, *The Holocaust: The Jewish Tragedy* (London, St Edmundsbury Press, 1986), p.

2. In Poland the Jewish population of most major cities was one third Jewish. In many smaller cities Jews comprised 50% to 70% of the population. http://www.info.kalisz.pl/Statut/JewsWar2.htm.

In Poland and other parts of Eastern Europe, if you were able to escape to the forests you also had to avoid the local population as they would actively hunt for Jews. If found, you were either killed by the locals or turned over to the Nazis for a bounty.

3. Michael Berenbaum, unpublished essay on resistance.

4. *Ibid.*

5. Nechama Tec, *Defiance: The Bielski Partisans* (Lanham, MD: University Press, 1993), p. 82.

6. Israel Gutman, *Resistance: The Warsaw Ghetto Uprising* (New York: Houghton Mifflin Books, 1998), p. 103 .

7. Jeanette Friedman, interview with author, August 2006.

8. Chana Mlotek, *Mir Trogen a Gezang* (New York: Workmen's Circle, 1972), p. 190.

9. Interview with Peska Friedman, November 1979. See also Hillel Seidman, *The Warsaw Ghetto Diary*, trans. by Yosef Israel (Jerusalem: Targum Press, 1997).

CHAPTER ELEVEN: DENIAL IS NOT A RIVER IN EGYPT

1. As quoted in Richard G. Hovannisian, *Remembrance and Denial: The Case of the Armenian Genocide* (Detroit, MI: Wayne State University Press, 1999) p. 287.

2. http://www.ushmm.org/wlc/article.php?lang =en&ModuleId=10006131

3. As quoted in Pablo De Greiff, *Handbook of Reparations: The International Center for Transitional Justice* (New York: Oxford University Press, 2006,) p. 427.

4. Michael Shermer and Alex Grobman, *Denying History: Who says the Holocaust Never Happened and Why Do They Say It* (Berkeley: University of California Press, 2000), p 1ff.

5. D. D. Guttenplan, *The Holocaust on Trial* (New York: W. W. Norton & Company, 2001), p. 3.
"In an American court Irving would have to prove that what Lipstadt wrote about him was false; he also would have to prove that she knew it was false. In Britain the libel laws favor the person suing. Here it would be up to Lipstadt to prove that what she wrote was true. And since Irving claimed that he couldn't be described as a 'Holocaust denier' because the gas chambers themselves were a hoax, Lipstadt and her lawyers were, in effect, forced to prove the reality of the Holocaust."

6. "Holocaust Denier is Jailed," BBC News," February 20, 2006. http://news.bbc.co.uk/2/hi/europe/4733820.stm

Holocaust denial is illegal in many European countries. Some countries have laws against libel or the incitement of racial hatred. Other countries like Canada and the United Kingdom do not have specific laws against Holocaust denial. David Irving was arrested in Austria and eventually convicted of "glorifying and identifying with the German Nazi Party" which is a crime in Austria. The European Union has not prohibited Holocaust denial outright, a maximum term of three years in jail is the usual option. What is illegal is "denying or grossly trivializing crimes of genocide, crimes against humanity and war crimes." In the United States,

Holocaust denial is protected by the First Amendment to
the US Constitution.

7. Alex Grobman, "Justice at long last served," *The Jewish
Independent*, March 3, 2006.

8. *Der Spiegel* online, "Pity for this Man is Out
of Place" February 2, 2006. http://www.spiegel.de/
international/0,1518,402404,00.html

9. Jeanette Friedman, "Overcoming the Maxwell Factor,"
Lifestyles Magazine, Pre-Spring Issue, 1996, pp. 28-32.

10. The Vatican online http://www.vatican.va/holy_father/
benedict_xvi/speeches/2009/may/documents/hf_ben-
xvi_spe_20090515_farewell-tel-aviv_en.html

11. Manya Brachear, "Who wins in interfaith relations?"
ChicagoTribune.com, February 3, 2009, /newsblogs.
chicagotribune.com/religion_theseeker/2009/02/who-
wins-in-interfaith-relations.html.

12. "Holocaust deniers 'not Catholic': Israel nuncio," CN
CathNews, March 11, 2009.

13. Associated Press, "Cardinal Mahony Bans Holocaust
Denier From L.A. Archdiocese, *USA Today*, March 4, 2009,
http://www.usatoday.com/news/religion/2009-03-04-
mahony-williamson-holocaust_N.htm

14. Jonny Paul, "UK Christian, Muslim Leaders Join Chief
Rabbi on Visit to Auschwitz," *The Jerusalem Post*, November
13, 2008.

15. BBC News, March 15, 2002, Saudi Police 'Stopped' Fire
Rescue. http://news.bbc.co.uk/2/hi/middle_east/1874471.
stm

16. Yehuda Bauer, Jerusalem Center for Public Affairs
http://www.jcpa.org/JCPA/Templates/ShowPage.asp?

DRIT=3&DBID=1&LNGID=1&TMID=111&FID=624&PID
=0&IID=2927&TTL=Reviewing_the_Holocaust_Anew_in_
Multiple_Contexts

CHAPTER TWELVE: STORIES OF SURVIVAL

1. Simon Wiesenthal, *Justice Not Vengeance* (London: Wiedenfeld & Nicholson, 1989), p. 351.

2. Peska Friedman, *Going Forward* (New York: Artscroll, 1998).

3. Ernest W. Michel, *Promises to Keep: One Mans Journey Against Incredible Odds* (Ft. Lee, NJ: Barricade Books, 1993), p1ff.

NOTES FOR A CONCISE HISTORY OF THE HOLOCAUST

1. The Yellow Star set Jews apart as "the other" and marked them as an inferior race. The practice of forcing Jews and other non Muslims to wear distinctive clothes originated in Muslim lands as a result of the Pact of Omar in the ninth century. In Christian countries the Fourth Latrean Council, convened by Pope Innocent III in 1215 decreed that Jews living in Christian lands were forced to wear a distinctive badge on their clothing. This became the model for the Yellow Star that the Nazis used during the Holocaust.

2. See, Lev. iii. 17, vii. 26, xix. 26; Deut. xii. 16; I Sam. xiv. 32, 33; Ezek, xxxiii. 25; compare also Acts xv. 29.

3. Ellis Rivkin, Seymour Rossel, Robert M. Seltzer, ED, *Unity Principle: The Shaping of Jewish History* (Behrman House, Incorporated,January 2003) Rivkin explores how monotheism enabled Jews to adapt whenever they were confronted by new historical forces.

4. J. Michael Parker, "Professor Blames Twisted Ethics for Holocaust's Rise" *San Antonio Express-News*, February 12, 1995.

5. Bryan Mark Rigg, *Hitler's Jewish Soldiers: The Untold Story of Nazi Racial Laws and Men of Jewish Descent in the German Military*, (University Press of Kansas, 2002: Original from the University of Michigan) p.72.

"About 10,000 volunteered for duty, and over 100,000 out of a total German-Jewish population of 550,000 served during World War I. Some 78% saw front-line duty, 12,000 died in battle, over 30,000 received decorations, and 19,000 were promoted. Approximately 2,000 Jews became military officers and 1,200 became medical officers."

6. Lucy S, Dawidowicz, *The War Against The Jews: 1933-1945,*

(New York, Holt, Rinehart and Winston, 1974) p. 48-69.

On April 1, 1933, a week after Hitler became dictator of Germany, he ordered a boycott of Jewish shops, banks, offices and department stores. But the boycott was mostly ignored by German shoppers and was called off after three days. However, the unsuccessful boycott was followed by a rapid series of laws which robbed the Jews of many rights.

On April 7, "The Law of the Restoration of the Civil Service" was introduced which made 'Aryanism' a necessary requirement in order to hold a civil service position. All Jews holding such positions were dismissed or forced into retirement.

On April 22, Jews were prohibited from serving as patent lawyers and from serving as doctors in state-run insurance institutions.

On April 25, a law against the overcrowding of German schools placed severe limits on the number of young Jews allowed to enroll in public schools.

On May 6, the Civil Service law was amended to close loopholes in order to keep out honorary university professors, lecturers and notaries.

On June 2, a law prohibited Jewish dentists and dental technicians from working with state-run insurance institutions.

On September 28, all non-Aryans and their spouses were prohibited from government employment.

On September 29, Jews were banned from all cultural and entertainment activities including literature, art, film and theater.

In early October, Jews were prohibited from being journalists and all newspapers were placed under Nazi control.
http://www.historyplace.com/worldwar2/timeline/boycott.htm

7. USHMM, Book Burning, authors like Ernest Hemingway, Helen Keller, H.G. Wells, and Franz Kafka also had their books burned. Photos and historical film footage of Book

Burning available at http://www.ushmm.org/wlc/article.
php?ModuleId=10005852

8. Michael Berenbaum, s.v. Holocaust, www.Britannica.
com

9. *Ibid.*

10. Germany was not alone in sterilizing the disabled. In the
United States, forced sterilization of the "feebleminded" for
the "protection and health of the state" was legal in 18 states
and performed without the permission of the "patients."
More than 60,000 Americans were sterilized this way, and
the laws of eugenics that allowed this were upheld in 1927
by the U.S. Supreme Court. The policy did not end until the
early 1960s, as a result of legal challenges and the civil rights
movement.

11. For background of bringing "Euthanasia" to the Camps
see, Robert Jay Lifton, *The Nazi Doctors: Medical Killing and the
Psychology of Genocide*, (Basic Books, 1988), pp. 134-147.

12. *Op. cit.*, Dawidowicz, pp. 63-69.

13. David Clay Large, *Nazi Games: The Olympics of 1936*,
(W.W. Norton, New York, 2007). The author describes the
indifference to Hitler's persecution of the Jews and the
insistence of American Olympic Committee, headed by
Avery Brundage, that the games be played in Berlin despite
the enactment of the Nuremberg Laws, which deprived
Germany's Jews of their citizenship. p. 1ff.

14. Jack R. Fischel, *The Holocaust*, (Westport, Connecticut,
Greenwood Publishing Group, March 1998). For details on
the Jewish reaction to the Nuremberg Laws and Emigration
from Germany see pp. 24-27.

15. *Manchester Guardian*, May 21, 1939, p. 8. James Rothschild,
a Liberal member of Parliament during the debates, said that
"for the majority of Jews who go to Palestine it is a question
of migration or physical extermination."

16. Martin Gilbert, *Kristallnacht: Prelude to Destruction*, (New York: HarperCollins, 2006). Through more than 50 eyewitness testimonies Martin Gilbert describes the terror that began with the onset of the Night of Broken Glass as *Kristallnacht* was known.

17. Ron Roizen, "Herschel Grynszpan: the Fate of A Forgotten Assassin," *Holocaust and Genocide Studies*, Vol. 1, No.2. (1986): pp. 217-228.

18. According to the USHMM between 1933 and 1945, Nazi Germany established about 20,000 camps to imprison millions of victims, http://www.ushmm.org/wlc/article. php?lang=en&ModuleId=10005144

19. For background on Einsatzgruppen (Mobile Killing Units), see the USHMM web site, http://www.ushmm.org/ wlc/article.php?ModuleId=10005130

20. For background on the Wannsee Conference and the Final Solution, see the USHMM web site http://www.ushmm. org/wlc/article.php?lang=en&ModuleId=10005477#Relat edArticles

21. Memorial and Museum Auschwitz-Birkenau, Kl Auschwitz-Birkenau: A History of the Camp, http:// www.auschwitz.org.pl/new/let_my_people_live/forum/ www.auschwitzanniversary2005.pl/index-eng6a4f. html?s2=articles&s3=auschwitz

22. Christopher R. Browning, *Ordinary Men: Reserve Police Battalion 101 and the Final Solution in Poland* (New York: HarperPerennial, 1998), P. XV.

23. Yad Vashem, http://www1.yadvashem.org/righteous_ new/statistics_main.html

24. David Harry Bennett, *The Party of Fear: From Nativist Movements to the New Right in American History*, p. 269. Bennett maintains that aside from issues of antisemitism in the State Department, Breckinridge Long was an antisemite.

25. Robert W. Kesting, *The Black Experience During the Holocaust: In The Holocaust and History: The Known, the Unknown, the Disputed, and the Reexamined*, edited by Michael Berenbaum and Abraham J. Peck (Bloomington: Indiana University Press, 1998), pp. 358-365.

26. *Ibid.*, p. 361.

27. Raul Hilberg, *The Destruction of the European Jews* Vol. 3, (New York: Holmes and Meier, 1985). p. 1201-2.

Most of the published estimates are between five and six million Jews that were killed. The original number of six million is attributed to Eichmann and is quoted by the International Military Tribunal, in Germany in September 30, 1946. After the war The Institute for Jewish Affairs in New York City made their own determination as follows. "the death toll was 5,659,600 to 5,673,100, including 1,250,000 within the August 1939 boundaries of the USSR. The Soviet share was based on the assumption that originally there had been 2,100,000 Jewish inhabitants in that portion of the old territory which was to be occupied by the Germans, that Soviet authorities had evacuated half of the urban residents but a smaller percentage of the village population from this region, and that there was a residue of 30,000 survivors. These numbers are primarily from an actual account of the victims. They fall into three categories, death through hunger and disease in ghettos, shootings and deportation to death camps.

28. USHMM, Jehovah's Witnesses: Persecution 1870-1936, http://www.ushmm.org/wlc/article. php?lang=en&ModuleId=10005433

29. Sonke Neitzel, *Tapping Hitler's Generals: Transcripts Of Secret Conversations 1942-45*. London, Greenhill Books, 2007. See also Andrew Roberts, "The Genocide Generals: secret recordings explode the myth they knew nothing about the Holocaust," Mail Online, July 21, 2007. http:// www.dailymail.co.uk/femail/article-469883/The-

Genocide-Generals-secret-recordings-explode-myth-knew-Holocaust.html

30. Deborah Sontag and Alessandra Stanley, "Ending the Pilgramage, the Pope Asks God for Brotherhood," *New York Times*, March 27, 2000. See also http://www.nytimes.com/1986/04/14/international/europe/14POPE.html

I have learned that bigotry and hatred are not the real dangers. The real evil is that there are those who know the problem and are silent onlookers.

Rabbi Joachim Prinz

For tolerance cannot be assumed, it has to be taught again and again. We must instill in our children that hate is never right, and love is never wrong."

Dwight D. Eisenhower

APPENDICES

APPENDIX ONE
ঙৃৎঌ

THE NUREMBERG LAWS

Nazi Racial Legislation: The Nuremberg Laws

One of the earliest statements of the Nazi Party—the policy document of 1920 known as the *Twenty-Five Points*—explicitly foreshadowed the exclusion of Jews from German citizenship (Point 4).Thus, as soon as Hitler came to power in 1933, no time was lost in proceeding against Germany's Jewish citizens. In the early months of the regime, they were prey to unbridled violence by Party activists during the so-called Brown Terror. Officially, steps were immediately taken to dismiss Jews from the civil service, reduce their number in the professions, and curtail the students in schools and colleges. Partly as a ploy to bring order to the shameless Party activism against inoffensive citizens and to clarify the regime's attitude to German Jewry, the two measures outlined below were passed at a meeting of the Party Congress at Nuremberg on Sept. 15, 1935.

Two of the laws are outlined below. The third, the Reich Flag Act, decreed the new German national flag to be the Nazi swastika flag.

Law for the Protection of German Blood and German Honor

Firm in the knowledge that the purity of German blood is the basis for the survival of the German people and inspired by the unshakeable determination to safeguard the future of the German nation, the Reichstag has unanimously resolved upon the following law, which is promulgated herewith:

Section 1

Marriages between Jews and citizens of German or some

related blood are forbidden. Such marriages contracted despite the law are invalid, even if they take place abroad in order to avoid the law.

Section 2

Sexual relations outside marriage between Jews and citizens of German or related blood are forbidden.

Section 3

Jews will not be permitted to employ female citizens of German or related blood who are under 45 years as housekeepers.

Section 4

1. Jews are forbidden to raise the national flag or display the national colors.

2. However, they are allowed to display the Jewish colors. The exercise of this right is protected by the State.

Section 5

1. Anyone who disregards Section 1 is liable to penal servitude.

2. Anyone who disregards the prohibition of Section 2 will be punished with imprisonment or penal servitude.

3. Anyone who disregards the provisions of Sections 3 or 4 will be punished with imprisonment up to one year or with a fine, or with one of these penalties.

The Reich Citizenship Law, 1935
Article 1

Section 1

A German subject is one who is a member of the protective union of the German Reich and is bound to it by special obligations. . . .

Section 2

1. A Reich citizen is that subject who is of German or related blood only and who through his behavior demonstrates that he is ready and able to serve faithfully the German people and Reich.

2. The right to citizenship of the Reich is acquired by the grant of citizenship papers.

3. A citizen of the Reich is the sole bearer of full political rights as provided by the law.

In the subsequent clarifying regulation of Nov. 14, 1935, a Jew was defined as anyone who was descended from: (a) at least three racially full Jewish grandparents or (b) two full Jewish parents if he or she belonged to the Jewish religious community (i.e., an observing Jew); was married to a Jewish person; was the offspring of a full Jew (as defined in a.) or the offspring of an extramarital relationship with a full Jew. Neither could a Jew be a citizen of the Reich, vote or hold public office.

Incidentally, persons of mixed Jewish blood (i.e., half-Jews — with one or two Jewish grandparents) were absolved from these restrictions, though, again, Jewish observance tightened the restrictions.

APPENDIX TWO
ҩ∾ҩ

THE SIX PILLARS OF CHARACTER
JOSEPHSON INSTTITUTE OF ETHICS
www.charactercounts.org

Trustworthiness

Be honest • Don't deceive, cheat or steal • Be reliable — do what you say you'll do • Have the courage to do the right thing • Build a good reputation • Be loyal — stand by your family, friends and country

Respect

Treat others with respect; follow the Golden Rule • Be tolerant of differences • Use good manners, not bad language • Be considerate of the feelings of others • Don't threaten, hit or hurt anyone • Deal peacefully with anger, insults and disagreements

Responsibility

Do what you are supposed to do • Persevere: keep on trying! • Always do your best • Use self-control • Be self-disciplined • Think before you act — consider the consequences • Be accountable for your choices

Fairness

Play by the rules • Take turns and share • Be open-minded; listen to others • Don't take advantage of others • Don't blame others carelessly

Caring

Be kind • Be compassionate and show you care • Express gratitude • Forgive others • Help people in need

Citizenship

Do your share to make your school and community better • Cooperate • Get involved in community affairs • Stay informed; vote • Be a good neighbor • Obey laws and rules • Respect authority • Protect the environment

APPENDIX THREE
୧୬

DEFINITION OF A SOCIOPATH
AN EVIL PERSON
Profile of the Sociopath

(These traits are based on the psychopathy checklists of H. Cleckley and R. Hare.)

Some of the common features of descriptions of the behavior of sociopaths.

- Glibness and Superficial Charm

- Manipulative and Cunning

   They never recognize the rights of others and see their self-serving behaviors as permissible. They appear to be charming, yet are covertly hostile and domineering, seeing their victim as merely an instrument to be used. They may dominate and humiliate their victims.

- Grandiose Sense of Self

   Feels entitled to certain things as "their right."

- Pathological Lying

   Has no problem lying coolly and easily and it is almost impossible for them to be truthful on a consistent basis. Can create, and get caught up in, a complex belief about their own powers and abilities. Extremely convincing and even able to pass lie detector tests.

- Lack of Remorse, Shame or Guilt

A deep seated rage, which is split off and repressed, is at their core. Does not see others around them as people, but only as targets and opportunities. Instead of friends, they have victims and accomplices who end up as victims. The end always justifies the means and they let nothing stand in their way.

- Shallow Emotions

When they show what seems to be warmth, joy, love and compassion it is more feigned than experienced and serves an ulterior motive. Outraged by insignificant matters, yet remaining unmoved and cold by what would upset a normal person. Since they are not genuine, neither are their promises.

- Incapacity for Love

- Need for Stimulation

Living on the edge. Verbal outbursts and physical punishments are normal. Promiscuity and gambling are common.

- Callousness/Lack of Empathy

Unable to empathize with the pain of their victims, having only contempt for others' feelings of distress and readily taking advantage of them.

- Poor Behavioral Controls/Impulsive Nature

Rage and abuse, alternating with small expressions of love and approval produce an addictive cycle for abuser and abused, as well as creating hopelessness in the victim. Believe they are all-powerful, all-knowing, entitled to every wish, no sense of personal boundaries, no concern for their impact on others.

- Early Behavior Problems/Juvenile Delinquency

  Usually has a history of behavioral and academic difficulties, yet "gets by" by conning others. Problems in making and keeping friends; aberrant behaviors such as cruelty to people or animals, stealing, etc.

- Irresponsibility/Unreliability

  Not concerned about wrecking others' lives and dreams. Oblivious or indifferent to the devastation they cause. Does not accept blame themselves, but blames others, even for acts they obviously committed.

- Promiscuous Sexual Behavior/Infidelity

  Promiscuity, child sexual abuse, rape and sexual acting out of all sorts.

- Lack of Realistic Life Plan/Parasitic Lifestyle Tends to move around a lot or makes all encompassing promises for the future, poor work ethic but exploits others effectively.

- Criminal or Entrepreneurial Versatility

Changes their image as needed to avoid prosecution. Changes life story readily.

Other Related Qualities:

1. Contemptuous of those who seek to understand them

2. Does not perceive that anything is wrong with them

3. Authoritarian

4. Secretive

5. Paranoid

6. Only rarely in difficulty with the law, but seeks out situations where their tyrannical behavior will be tolerated, condoned, or admired

7. Conventional appearance

8. Goal is enslavement of their victim(s)

9. Exercises despotic control over every aspect of the victim's life

10. Has an emotional need to justify their crimes and therefore needs their victim's affirmation (respect, gratitude and love)

11. Ultimate goal is the creation of a willing victim

12. Incapable of real human attachment to another

13. Unable to feel remorse or guilt

14. Extreme narcissism and grandiose

15. May state readily that their goal is to rule the world (The above traits are based on the psychopathy checklists of H. Cleckley and R. Hare.)

NOTE: In the 1830's this disorder was called "moral insanity." By 1900 it was changed to "psychopathic personality." More recently it has been termed "antisocial personality disorder" in the DSM-III and DSM-IV. Some critics have complained that, in the attempt to rely only on 'objective' criteria, the DSM has broadened the concept to include too many individuals. The APD category includes people who commit illegal, immoral or self-serving acts for a variety of reasons and are not necessarily psychopaths.

APPENDIX FOUR

THE PHYSICIANS' OATH

As a result of the Holocaust, the World Medical Association in Geneva established a physician's oath in 1948.

- I solemnly pledge myself to consecrate my life to the service of humanity;

- I will give to my teachers the respect and gratitude which is their due;

- I will practice my profession with conscience and dignity; the health of my patient will be my first consideration;

- I will maintain by all the means in my power, the honor and the noble traditions of the medical profession; my colleagues will be my brothers;

- I will not permit considerations of religion, nationality, race, party politics or social standing to intervene between my duty and my patient;

- I will maintain the utmost respect for human life from the time of conception, even under threat, I will not use my medical knowledge contrary to the laws of humanity;

- I make these promises solemnly, freely and upon my honor.

APPENDIX FIVE

ა∞ა

REMARKS BY PRESIDENT OBAMA,
GERMAN CHANCELLOR MERKEL,
AND ELIE WIESEL
AT BUCHENWALD CONCENTRATION CAMP,
WEIMAR, GERMANY. June 5, 2009

CHANCELLOR MERKEL: (As translated.) Mr. President, ladies and gentlemen. Here in this place a concentration camp was established in 1937. Not far from here lies Lima, a place where Germans created wonderful works of art, thereby contributing to European culture and civ il ization. Not far from that place where once artists, poets, and great minds met, terror, violence, and tyranny reigned over this camp.

At the beginning of our joint visit to the Buchenwald memorial the American President and I stood in front of a plaque commemorating all the victims. When you put your hand on the memorial you can feel that it has warmed up — it is kept at a temperature of 37 degrees, the body temperature of a living human being. This, however, was not a place for living, but a place for dying.

Unimaginable horror, shock — there are no words to adequately describe what we feel when we look at the suffering inflicted so cruelly upon so many people here and in other concentration and extermination camps under National Socialist terror. I bow my head before the victims.

We, the Germans, are faced with the agonizing question how and why — how could this happen? How could Germany wreak such havoc in Europe and the world? It is therefore incumbent upon us Germans to show an unshakeable resolve to do everything we can so that something like this never happens again.

On the 25th of January, the presidents of the associations of former inmates at the concentration camps presented their request to the public, and this request closes with the following words: "The last eyewitness appeal to Germany, to all European states, and to the international community to continue preserving and honoring the human gift of remembrance and commemoration into the future. We ask young people to carry on our struggle against Nazi ideology, and for a just, peaceful and tolerant world; a world that has no place for anti-Semitism, racism, xenophobia, and right-wing extremism."

This appeal of the survivors clearly defines the very special responsib il ity we Germans have to shoulder with regard to our history. And for me, therefore, there are three messages that are important today. First, let me emphasize, we Germans see it as past of our country's raison d'être to keep the everlasting memory alive of the break with civ il ization that was the Shoah. Only in this way w il l we be able to shape our future.

I am therefore very grateful that the Buchenwald memorial has always placed great emphasis on the dialogue with younger people, to conversations with eyewitnesses, to documentation, and a broad-based educational program.

Second, it is most important to keep the memory of the great sacrifices alive that had to be made to put an end to the terror of National Socialism and to liberate its victims and to rid all people of its yoke.

This is why I want to say a particular word of gratitude to the President of the United States of America , Barack Obama, for visiting this particular memorial. It gives me an opportunity to align yet again that we Germans shall never forget, and we owe the fact that we were given the opportunity after the war to start anew, to enjoy peace and freedom to the resolve, the strenuous efforts, and indeed to a sacrifice made in blood of the United States of America and of all those who stood by your side as allies or fighters in the resistance.

We were able to find our place again as members of the international community through a forward-looking partnership. And this partnership was finally key to enabling us to overcome the painful division of our country in 1989, and the division also of our continent. Today we remember the victims of this place. This includes remembering the victims of the so-called Special Camp 2, a detention camp run by the Soviet military administration from 1945 to 1950. Thousands of people perished due to the inhumane conditions of their detention.

Third, here in Buchenwald I would like to highlight an obligation placed on us Germans as a consequence of our past: to stand up for human rights, to stand up for rule of law, and for democracy. We shall fight against terror, extremism, and anti-Semitism. And in the awareness of our responsib il ity we shall strive for peace and freedom, together with our friends and partners in the United States and all over the world.

PRESIDENT OBAMA: Chancellor Merkel and I have just finished our tour here at Buchenwald. I want to thank Dr. Volkhard Knigge, who gave an outstanding account of what we were witnessing. I am particularly grateful to be accompanied by my friend Elie Wiesel, as well as Mr. Bertrand Herz, both of whom are survivors of this place.

We saw the area known as Little Camp where Elie and Bertrand were sent as boys. In fact, at the place that commemorates this camp, there is a photograph in which we can see a 16-year-old Elie in one of the bunks along with the others. We saw the ovens of the crematorium, the guard towers, the barbed wire fences, the foundations of barracks that once held people in the most unimaginable conditions.

We saw the memorial to all the survivors—a steel plate, as Chancellor Merkel said, that is heated to 37 degrees Celsius, the temperature of the human body; a reminder—where people were deemed inhuman because of their differences —of the mark that we all share.

Now these sights have not lost their horror with the passage of time. As we were walking up, Elie said, "if these trees could talk." And there's a certain irony about the beauty of the landscape and the horror that took place here.

More than half a century later, our grief and our outrage over what happened have not diminished. I will not forget what I've seen here today.

I've known about this place since I was a boy, hearing stories about my great uncle, who was a very young man serving in World War II. He was part of the 89th Infantry Division, the first Americans to reach a concentration camp. They liberated Ohrdruf, one of Buchenwald 's sub-camps.

And I told this story, he returned from his service in a state of shock saying little and isolating himself for months on end from family and friends, alone with the painful memories that would not leave his head. And as we see—as we saw some of the images here, it's understandable that someone who witnessed what had taken place here would be in a state of shock.

My great uncle's commander, General Eisenhower, under-stood this impulse to s il ence. He had seen the piles of bodies and starving survivors and deplorable conditions that the American soldiers found when they arrived, and he knew that those who witnessed these things might be too stunned to speak about them or be able—be unable to find the words to describe them; that they might be rendered mute in the way my great uncle had. And he knew that what had happened here was so unthinkable that after the bodies had been taken away, that perhaps no one would believe it.

And that's why he ordered American troops and Germans from the nearby town to tour the camp. He invited congressmen and journalists to bear witness and ordered photographs and f il ms to be made. And he insisted on viewing every corner of these camps so that—and I quote —he could "be in a position to give first-hand evidence of these things if ever in the future there develops a tendency to charge these allegations merely to propaganda."

We are here today because we know this work is not yet finished. To this day, there are those who insist that the Holocaust never happened—a denial of fact and truth that is baseless and ignorant and hateful. This place is the ultimate rebuke to such thoughts; a reminder of our duty to confront those who would tell lies about our history.

Also to this day, there are those who perpetuate every form of intolerance—racism, anti-Semitism, homophobia, xenophobia, sexism, and more—hatred that degrades its victims and diminishes us all. In this century, we've seen genocide. We've seen mass graves and the ashes of v il lages burned to the ground; ch il dren used as soldiers and rape used as a weapon of war. This places teaches us that we must be ever vig il ant about the spread of ev il in our own time, that we must reject the false comfort that others' suffering is not our problem and commit ourselves to resisting those who would subjugate others to serve their own interests.

But as we reflect today on the human capacity for ev il and our shared obligation to defy it, we're also reminded of the human capacity for good. For amidst the countless acts of cruelty that took place here, we know that there were many acts of courage and kindness, as well. The Jews who insisted on fasting on Yom Kippur. The camp cook who hid potatoes in the lining of his prison uniform and distributed them to his fellow inmates, risking his own life to help save theirs. The prisoners who organized a special effort to protect the ch il dren here, sheltering them from work and giving them extra food. They set up secret classrooms, some of the inmates, and taught history and math and urged the children to think about their future professions. And we were just hearing about the resistance that formed and the irony that the base for the resistance was in the latrine areas because the guards found it so offensive that they wouldn't go there. And so out of the filth, that became a space in which small freedoms could thrive.

When the American GIs arrived they were astonished to find more than 900 children still alive, and the youngest was just three years old. And I'm told that a couple of the prisoners even wrote a Buchenwald song that many here sang. Among the lyrics were these: "...whatever our fate, we will say yes to life, for the day will come when we are free...in our blood we carry the will to live and in our hearts, in our hearts—faith."

These individuals never could have known the world would one day speak of this place. They could not have known that some of them would live to have children and grandchildren who would grow up hearing their stories and would return here so many years later to find a museum and memorials and the clock tower set permanently to 3:15, the moment of liberation.

They could not have known how the nation of Israel would rise out of the destruction of the Holocaust and the strong, enduring bonds between that great nation and my own. And they could not have known that one day an American President would visit this place and speak of them and that he would do so standing side by side with the German Chancellor in a Germany that is now a vibrant democracy and a valued American ally.

They could not have known these things. But still surrounded by death they willed themselves to hold fast to life. In their hearts they still had faith that evil would not triumph in the end, that whil e history is unknowable it arches towards progress, and that the world would one day remember them. And it is now up to us, the living, in our work, wherever we are, to resist injustice and intolerance and indifference in whatever forms they may take, and ensure that those who were lost here did not go in vain. It is up to us to redeem

that faith. It is up to us to bear witness; to ensure that the
world continues to note what happened here; to remember
all those who survived and all those who perished, and to
remember them not just as victims, but also as individuals
who hoped and loved and dreamed just like us.

And just as we identify with the victims, it's also important
for us I think to remember that the perpetrators of such ev
il were human, as well, and that we have to guard against
cruelty in ourselves. And I want to express particular thanks
to Chancellor Merkel and the German people, because it's
not easy to look into the past in this way and acknowledge
it and make something of it, make a determination that they
w il l stand guard against acts like this happening again.

Rather than have me end with my remarks I thought it was
appropriate to have Elie Wiesel provide some reflection and
some thought as he returns here so many years later to the
place where his father died.

MR. WIESEL: Mr. President, Chancellor Merkel, Bertrand,
ladies and gentlemen. As I came here today it was actually
a way of coming and visit my father's grave — but he had no
grave. His grave is somewhere in the sky. This has become
in those years the largest cemetery of the Jewish people.

The day he died was one of the darkest in my life. He
became sick, weak, and I was there. I was there when he
suffered. I was there when he asked for help, for water. I
was there to receive his last words. But I was not there when
he called for me, although we were in the same block; he on
the upper bed and I on the lower bed. He called my name,
and I was too afraid to move. All of us were. And then he
died. I was there, but I was not there.

And I thought one day I w il l come back and speak to him,
and tell him of the world that has become mine. I speak to
him of times in which memory has become a sacred duty
of all people of good will — in America, where I live, or in
Europe or in Germany, where you, Chancellor Merkel, are

a leader with great courage and moral aspirations.

What can I tell him that the world has learned? I am not so sure. Mr. President, we have such high hopes for you because you, with your moral vision of history, will be able and compelled to change this world into a better place, where people will stop waging war—every war is absurd and meaningless; where people will stop hating one another; where people will hate the otherness of the other rather than respect it.

But the world hasn't learned. When I was liberated in 1945, April 11, by the American army, somehow many of us were convinced that at least one lesson will have been learned —that never again will there be war; that hatred is not an option, that racism is stupid; and the will to conquer other people's minds or territories or aspirations, that will is meaningless.

I was so hopeful. Paradoxically, I was so hopeful then. Many of us were, although we had the right to give up on humanity, to give up on culture, to give up on education, to give up on the possib il ity of living one's life with dignity in a world that has no place for dignity.

We rejected that possibility and we said, no, we must continue believing in a future, because the world has learned. But again, the world hasn't. Had the world learned, there would have been no Cambodia and no Rwanda and no Darfur and no Bosnia.

Will the world ever learn? I think that is why Buchenwald is so important—as important, of course, but differently as Auschwitz . It's important because here the big camp was a kind of international community. People came there from all horizons—political, economic, culture. The first globalization essay, experiment, were made in Buchenwald And all that was meant to diminish the humanity of human beings.

You spoke of humanity, Mr. President. Though unto us, in

those times, it was human to be inhuman. And now the world has learned, I hope. And of course this hope includes so many of what now would be your vision for the future. A sense of security for Israel, a sense of security for its neighbors, to bring peace in that place. The time must come. It's enough—enough to go to cemeteries, enough to weep for oceans. It's enough. There must come a moment—a moment of bringing people together.

And therefore we say anyone who comes here should go back with that resolution. Memory must bring people together rather than set them apart. Memories here not to sow anger in our hearts, but on the contrary, a sense of solidarity that all those who need us. What else can we do except invoke that memory so that people everywhere who say the 21st century is a century of new beginnings, f il led with promise and infinite hope, and at times profound gratitude to all those who believe in our task, which is to improve the human condition.

A great man, Camus, wrote at the end of his marvelous novel, *The Plague*: "After all," he said, "after the tragedy, never the rest...there is more in the human being to celebrate than to denigrate." Even that can be found as truth—painful as it is—in Buchenwald.

Thank you, Mr. President, for allowing me to come back to my father's grave, which is still in my heart.

BIBLIOGRAPHY

Studying the Holocaust is very challenging, the most important criteria is the commitment to spend time to gain an understanding of the material. We urge that an integral part of studying the Holocaust is to hear the testimony of survivors and other eyewitnesses. Above all we recommend that you visit to the United States Holocaust Memorial Museum in Washington.

Arendt, Hannah. *Eichmann in Jerusalem: A Report on the Banality of Evil.* New York: Penguin Classics, 1992

Balakian, Grigoris. *Armenian Golgotha: A Memoir of the Armenian Genocide, 1915-1918.* New York: Knopf, 2009.

Bardakjian, Kevork B. *Hitler and the Armenian Genocide.* Toronto: Zoryan Institute, 1985.
An argument is made that the failure to bring the Ottoman Empire to justice for the crimes against the Armenians led Hitler to believe that he would not be held responsible for his acts of Genocide.

Bauer, Yehuda, *Jews For Sale? Nazi-Jewish Negotiations, 1933-1945.* New Haven: Yale University Press, 1994.
_____. *A History of the Holocaust.* New York: Franklin Watts, 1982.
_____, and Nathan Rotenstreich. *The Holocaust as Historical Experience: Essays and a Discussion.* Teaneck, NJ: Holmes & Meier, 1981.

Beker, Sonia. *Symphony on Fire*. New Milford, NJ: The Wordsmithy, 2007.

Berenbaum, Michael, and Abraham Peck, eds., *The Holocaust and History: The Known, the Unknown, the Disputed, and the Reexamined*. Bloomington, IN: Indiana University Press, 1998.

Boren, Adam. *Journey Through the Inferno*. Washington, D.C.: United States Holocaust Memorial Museum and the Holocaust Survivors' Memoirs Project, in association with the World Federation of Bergen Belsen Association Inc., 2004.

Browning, Christopher R. *Ordinary Men: Reserve Police Battalion 101 and the Final Solution in Poland*. San Francisco: HarperCollins, 1993.

Card, Orson Scott. *Empire*. New York: Tor, 2006.

Cohn, Norman. *Warrant for Genocide*. UK: Serif, 2006.

Cord, Edith. *Becoming Edith*. New Milford, NJ: The Wordsmithy, 2008.

Dawidowicz, Lucy S. *The War Against the Jews, 1933-1945*. New York: Holt, Rinehart, and Winston, 1975.

Drucker, Malka. *Rescuers: Portraits of Moral Courage in the Holocaust*. Teaneck, NJ: Holmes & Meier, 1992.

Finger, Seymour, Maxwell, ed. *The Goldberg Commission Report: American Jewry During The Holocaust*. Reprinted by New Milford, NJ: The Wordsmithy, 2008.

Fogelman, Eva. *Conscience and Courage: Rescuers of Jews During the Holocaust*. New York: Anchor Doubleday, 1994.
_____. "Ideology and Individual Police Officers as Offenders, Resisters and Helpers During the Nazi Period in Germany." Speech delivered at Hochschule fur Polizei Villingen-Schwenningen.

Fermaglich, Kirsten. *American Dreams and Nazi Nightmares: Early Holocaust Consciousness and Liberal America, 1957-1965.* Lebanon, NH: University Press of New England, 2007.

Friedlander, Henry. *The Origins of Nazi Genocide: From Euthanasia to the Final Solution.* Chapel Hill, NC: The University of North Carolina Press, 1995.

Friedman, Ina R. "No Blacks Allowed," in *The Other Victims: First-Person Stories of Non-Jews Persecuted by the Nazis.* Boston: Houghton Mifflin, 1990, 91-93.

Friedman, Peska. *Going Forward.* New York: Artscroll, 1998.

Gilbert, Martin. *The Holocaust: A History of the Jews of Europe During the Second World War.* New York: Holt, Rinehart, and Winston, 1986.

Goldhagen, Daniel Jonah. *Hitler's Willing Executioners: Ordinary Germans and the Holocaust.* Vancouver, WA: Vintage Books, 1996.

Grobman. Alex. *Nations United.* AR: Balfour Books, 2006.
_____. *Battling for Souls.* Jersey City, NJ: Ktav, 2004.
_____. "Why Numbers Matter In Understanding The Shoah." Unpublished essay, 2009.

Gutman, Israel. *Resistance: The Warsaw Ghetto Uprising.* Boston: Houghton Mifflin Books, 1998.
_____, ed., *Encyclopedia of the Holocaust.* New York: Macmillan Publishing Company, 1990.

Guttenplan, D. D., *The Holocaust on Trial.* New York: W. W. Norton & Company, 2001.

Philip Hallie. *Lest Innocent Blood Be Shed: The Story of the Village of Le Chambon and How Goodness Happened There.* New York: Harper Perennial, 1994.

Helmreich, William. "Don't Look Back: Holocaust Survivors

in the U.S." October, 1991 http://www.jcpa.org/jl/hit17.
htm.

Josephson, Michael J. *Making Ethical Decisions*. Los Angeles:
Josephson Institute of Ethics, 1996.

Katz, Nathan. *Teach Us To Count Our Days*. New York:
Cornwall Press, 1999.

Kent, Roman. *Courage Was My Only Option: The Autobiography
of Roman Kent*. New York: Vantage Press, Inc, 2008.
_____, and Jeanette Friedman, *My Dog Lala*. Detroit, MI:
Teacher's Discovery, 2006.

Kesting, Robert W. "The Black Experience During the
Holocaust,"in *The Holocaust and History: The Known, the
Unknown, the Disputed, and the Reexamined*. eds. Michael
Berenbaum and Abraham J. Peck. Bloomington, IN: Indiana
University Press, 1998, 358-365.

Kranzler, David. *Holocaust Hero: Solomon Schonfeld*. Jersey
City, NJ: Ktav, 2004.

Laqueur, Walter, ed. *The Holocaust Encyclopedia*. New Haven,
CT: Yale University Press, 2001.

Lauterpacht, Elihu Sir. *International Law Reports*. Cambridge:
Cambridge University Press, 1999.

Lifton, Robert. *The Nazi Doctors: Medical Killing and the
Psychology of Genocide*. New York: Basic Books, 1986.

Lipstadt, Deborah. *Beyond Belief: The American Press and the
Coming of the Holocaust, 1933-1945*. New York: The Free Press,
1986.

Lozowick ,Yaacov. *Hitler's Bureaucrats: The Nazi Secret Police
and the Banality of Evil*. New York: Continuum, 2005.

Meed, Vladka. *On Both Sides of The Wall.* New York: Schocken Books, 1979.

Michel, Ernest W. *Promises to Keep: One Mans Journey Against Incredible Odds.* Ft. Lee, NJ: Barricade Books, 1993.

Milgram, Stanley. "The Milgram 'Shock' Experiment." *The Holocaust and Genocide: A Search for Conscience – An Anthology for Students.* Harry Furman, ed. New York: Anti-Defamation League, 1983.

Miller, Arthur G. *The Social Psychology of Good and Evil.* New York: Guilford Press, 2005.

Mlotek, Chana. *Mir Trogen a Gezang.* New York: Workmen's Circle, 1972.

New Jersey Commission on Holocaust Education. *The Holocaust and Genocide: The Betrayal of Humanity. Part I – A Curriculum Guide for Grades 9 –12. Vol. 1.* New Jersey: New Jersey Commission on Holocaust Education, 2003.

Peters, Thomas J. and Robert H. Waterman. *In Search of Excellence: Lessons from America's Best-Run Companies.* San Francisco: HarperCollins, 2004.

Rauschning, Hermann. *The Voice of Destruction: Conversations with Hitler 1940.* Whitefish, MT: Kessinger, 2004.

Rivkin, Ellis. *The Unity Principle: The Shaping of Jewish History.* Springfield, NJ: Behrman House, 2003.

Rosenthal, A.M., *Thirty-Eight Witnesses: The Kitty Genovese Case.* Los Angeles: University of California Press, 1999.

Robinson, Greg. *Order of the President: FDR and the Internment of Japanese Americans.* Boston: Harvard University Press, 2003.

Rosensaft, Hadassah Bimko. *Yesterday: My Story.* Holocaust

Survivors' Memoirs Project, Yad Vashem and Washington, D.C., 2004.

Rowling, J. K. *Harry Potter and the Deathly Hallows*. New York: Scholastic, 2007.

Rushkoff, Douglas. *Life, Inc.: How the World Became a Caorporation and How to Take It Back*. New York; Random House, 2009.

Schechter, Danny. *The More You Watch, The Less You Know*. New York: Seven Stories Press, 1998

Shapiro, Sonke. Tapping Hitler's Generals: Transcripts Of Secret *Conversations 1942-45*. London: Greenhill Books, 2007.

Shermer, Michael and Alex Grobman. *Denying History: Who says the Holocaust Never Happened and Why Do They Say It*. Los Angeles: University of California Press, 2000.

Singer, Flora M. *I was But a Child*. New York & Jerusalem: Yad Vashem, 2007.

Sternberg, Robert J., and Karin Sternberg. *The Nature of Hate*. Cambridge: Cambridge University Press, 2008.

Tec, Nechama. *Defiance, The Bielski Partisans*. New York: Oxford University Press, 1993.

Tenenbaum, Joseph F. *Legacy and Redemption: A Life Renewed*. Washington, D.C.: United States Holocaust Memorial Museum, 2004.

Taites, Emily, *Holocaust: A Biographical Dictionary*. Westport, CT: Greenwood Press, 2007)

Wade, Wayne Craig. *The Fiery Cross, The Ku Klux Klan in America*. New York: Simon and Schuster, 1987.

Wainwright, Louden. *The Dying Girl That No One Helped, The Holocaust and Genocide: A Search for Conscience — An Anthology for Students.* Harry Furman, ed. New York: Anti-Defamation League, 1983.

Waller, James. *Becoming Evil: How Ordinary People Commit Genocide and Mass Killing.* New York: Oxford University Press, 2005.

Weber, Lewis. The Holocaust Chronicle: A History in Words and Pictures. Lincolnwood, IL: Publications International, 2003.

Wiesel, Elie. *Night.* New York: Bantam Books, 1986.

Wesenthal, Simon *Justice Not Vengeance.* London: Wiedenfeld & Nicholson, 1989.

Wistrich, Robert S. *Antisemitism: The Longest Hatred.* New York: Pantheon, 1991.

Wrobel, Eta. *My Life My Way.* New Milford, NJ: The Wordsmithy and YIVO, 2006.

Ziemian, Joseph, *The Cigarette Sellers of Three Crosses Square.* Minneapolis, MN: Lerner Publications Co., 1975. Original from the University of Michigan. Digitized Aug 26, 2008.

NOTES ON USING
INTERNET SOURCES

Using the internet for research on the Holocaust can be problematic. We recommend that students link to reputable sites through USHMM, Yad Vashem or other organizations you know you can trust. Denier Web sites are crafted to appear as if they are authentic.

United States Holocaust Memorial Museum
The museum web site is the best source of information for the Holocaust on the Internet. The museum features many resources from online exhibits to original archival material, original artifacts and photos. There is also a section for teachers with online tutorials and sample lesson plans.
http://www.ushmm.org

Yad Vashem
The Holocaust Martyrs' and Heroes' Remembrance Authority" is Israel's official memorial to the Jewish victims of the Holocaust. Established in 1953, Yad Vashem has been entrusted with documenting the history of the Jewish people during the Holocaust, preserving the memory and story of each of the six million victims, and imparting the legacy of the Holocaust for generations to come through its archives, library, school, museums and recognition of the Righteous

Among the Nations.
http://www1.yadvashem.org

**GENOCIDE PREVENTION TASK FORCE REPORT
USHMM AND OTHERS**

http://www.ushmm.org/conscience/taskforce/report.
php

Simon Wiesenthal Center
http://www.wiesenthal.com

The Multimedia Learning Center. Offers online exhibitions
and teacher resources.
http://motlc.wiesenthal.com/

**University of Southern California Shoah Foundation
Institute**
The USC Shoah Foundation Institute for Visual History and
Education contains an archive of nearly 52,000 videotaped
testimonies from Holocaust survivors and other witnesses.
It is part of the College of Letters, Arts & Sciences at the
University of Southern California. The Foundation provides
educational services that reach educators, students, and the
general public around the world.
http://www.vhf.org

The Ghetto Fighters House
A place to visit to learn more about the Warsaw Ghetto
Uprising and educational programs and archives.
www.gfh.org.il/eng

Jewish Foundation for the Righteous
The Foundation was established to fulfill the traditional
Jewish commitment to hakarat hatov, the searching out and
recognition of goodness. The site offers access to testimonies,
and stories of non-Jewish rescuers during the Holocaust.
http://www.jfr.org

Anti-Defamation League
The nation's major civil rights/human relations agency and a
leader in the development of programs building bridges and
respect among diverse groups. A good resource for Teachers
to access material on the Holocaust.
http://www.adl.org/education/dimensions_18_2/
default.asp
A section is also available on denial.
http://www.adl.org/main_Holocaust/default.htm

State of New Jersey Commission on Holocaust Education
The center provides online curriculum guides on the
Holocaust. One of the best we have seen. Also available online
is an instructional guide Genocide in Darfur, Sudan.
http://www.state.nj.us/education/holocaust/

National Catholic Center for Holocaust Education
The Center counters antisemitism and fosters Catholic Jewish
Relations. The site provides a teaching guide for teaching
about the Holocaust in Catholic schools.
http://blogs.setonhill.edu/ncche/017824.php

The Chambon Foundation
Documents the rescue efforts of the residents in and around
Le Chambon-sur-Lignon, France, who risked their lives to
shelter 5,000 Jews, many of them children.
http://www.chambon.org/

Coolidge College German Propaganda Archive
http://www.calvin.edu/academic/cas/gpa/

Women and the Holocaust
Includes eyewitness accounts, book reviews, articles, essays,
poetry, and links to eyewitness testimonies and related
resources.
http://www.womenandtheholocaust.com/

Women and the Holocaust - New Jersey Council for the Humanities
Resource center for teachers that focuses on the experiences

of women. Presents lesson plans and suggested teaching methodologies
http://www.njch.org/holocaust/

The Genocide Intervention Network
http://www.genocideintervention.net/

Josephson Institute Center for Youth Ethics
Character counts is a great approach to the development of Character using the basic values of the "Six Pillars of Character" trustworthiness, respect, responsibility, fairness, caring and citizenship.
http://charactercounts.org/

Hiatt Collection of Holocaust Materials
Housed at the Dinand Library, College of the Holy Cross. Focuses on the role of the Roman Catholic Church and the Jesuit order during the Holocaust
http://www.holycross.edu/departments/library/website/hiatt/

Preventing Genocide
http://www.preventgenocide.org/prevent/scherrer.htm

Facing History and Ourselves
http://www.facinghistory.org/

Armenian National Institute
Web site of the Armenian National Institute dedicated to "the study, research and affirmation of the Armenian Genocide of the Ottoman Empire during World War I.
http://www.armenian-genocide.org/

Genocide Watch: The International Campaign to End Genocide
Formed to predict, prevent, stop, and punish genocide. Includes news articles, descriptions of acts of genocide in various regions.
http://www.genocidewatch.org/

Yale Center for International and Area Studies: Genocide Studies Program
Scholarly discussion and education about the Holocaust and genocide.
http://www.yale.edu/gsp/

Bosnia Documentary (film)
Explores the role of Serbian warlord Radovan Karadzic in the atrocities and genocide committed during the Bosnia
http://cgi.pbs.org/wgbh/pages/frontline/shows/karadzic/

Srebrenica: A Cry from the Grave (film)
Documentary about the massacre of over 7,000 civilians in Srebrenica, Bosnia, in July 1995.
http://www.pbs.org/wnet/cryfromthegrave/

The Triumph of Evil: How the West Ignored Warnings of the 1994 Rwanda Genocide and Turned its Back on the Victims
Contains a synopsis of the Rwandan genocide, suggested reading list, primary source documents, and information for educators; originally presented as part of the Frontline television program.
 http://www.pbs.org/wgbh/pages/frontline/shows/evil/

Holocaust Denial on Trial
Information on the trial of the David Irving v. Penguin Books and Deborah Lipstadt libel trial of January 2000.
http://www.holocaustdenialontrial.org

Gulf War Illnes Report
http://sph.bu.edu/insider/images/stories/resources/annual_reports/GWI%20and%20Health%20of%20GW%20Veterans_RAC-GWVI%20Report_2008.pdf

On-line Focus: Remembering the Past
Two people who have survived periods of horrific genocide have teamed up to speak about their experiences in the

Holocaust and Rwanda, with the hope of preventing such acts from happening again. Jeffrey Brown speaks to David Gewirtzman and Jacqueline Murekatete about their experiences and how they met.
http://www.pbs.org/newshour/bb/africa/jan-june04/genocide_04-09-04.html#

The Last Survivor, a very special movie about survivors of genocide
www.righteouspictures.com

Organizing at Your School to End the Genocide in Sudan
http://www.ushmm.org/conscience/alert/darfur/pdf/resource_kit.pdf

MUSIC URLS
Jake Taper and Marie Nelson, Is Corporate America to Blame for Hip-Hop Violence?, "Criminal Activity Becoming Rap Music's Selling Point". CBS News, April 22, 2005) http://abcnews.go.com/Nightline/News/story?id=694982&page=1

DMC On Violence In Hip-Hop: 'Something Has To Give', "After deaths of Proof, Jam Master Jay, veteran rapper wishes lyrics were more relevant, less violent", (MTV Networks, Apr 13, 2006)
http://www.mtv.com/news/articles/1528673/20060413/dmc.jhtml

Hearing criticizes sex, violence in hip-hop; Lawmakers, executives, rappers agree censorship isn't answer. MSNBC Tues., Sept. 25, 2007
http://www.msnbc.msn.com/id/20975017/

WEBSITES: Holocaust Music
http://fcit.usf.edu/holocaust/arts/music.htm
http://www.musicofremembrance.org/news/dec_11_07_concentration_camp.htm
http://www.ushmm.org/wlc/article.php?lang=en&ModuleId=10005416

http://www.remember.org/hist.root.music.html
http://www.pbs.org/independentlens/strangefruit/
protest.html
http://131.247.120.10/holocaust/arts/musVicti.htm

Civil Rights Music
http://folkmusic.about.com/od/toptens/tp/
Top10Protest.htm
http://www.cocojams.com/freedom_songs.htm
http://history.grand-forks.k12.nd.us/NDhistory/
LessonOverview.aspx?LessonID=316
http://www.voicesofcivilrights.org/civil5.html
http://www.lacarte.org/songs/anti-war/
http://www.brownielocks.com/sixtieswarsongs.html
http://www.cbsnews.com/stories/2006/12/12/opinion/
meyer/main2250923.shtml
www.comedycentral.com
http://www.youtube.com/watch?v=WmxT21uFRwM

SLAVERY
http://www.state.gov/g/tip/

STAR TREK EPISODES

LET THAT BE YOUR LAST BATTLEFIELD
http://www.imdb.com/video/cbs/vi2437218329

CITY ON THE EDGE OF FOREVER
http://www.theinsider.com/videos/1331426_Star_Trek_
The_City_on_the_Edge_of_Forever#

PATTERNS OF FORCE
http://www.fancast.com/tv/Star-
Trek/96413/620819805/Star-Trek:-The-Original-Series—
Patterns-of-Force/videos

Buy Red Saves Lives
http://www.joinred.com/Home.aspx

whyshouldicareontheweb.com

One Person can make a difference
http://www.one.org/

The UN Refuge Agency
http://www.unhcr.org/help/3f94ff664.html

Bill & Melinda Gates Foundation
http://www.gatesfoundation.org/Pages/home.aspx

The Auschwitz Museum
Research Advisory Committee on Gulf War Veterans'
Illnesses, Gulf War Illness and the Health of Gulf War
Veterans: Scientific Findings and Recommendations,
(Washington, D.C.: U.S. Government Printing Office,
November 2008)
www.auschwitz.org

SOCIAL ACTION
http://www.declareyourself.com

JOIN A GROUP THAT MAKES THINGS HAPPEN
http://socialaction.org

TWILIGHT ZONE: To Serve Man
http://www.youtube.com/watch?v=WudBfRa0ETw

http://www.cbs.com/classics/the_twilight_zone/
videovideo.php?cid=649562032&pid=W4F0L_skkbpXGUn
d7Qu3nO1bLGyk0Ihm&play=true&cc=2

Brothers under the skin.
http://www.imdb.com/video/cbs/vi2437218329

The Cherokee Trail of Tears – Oral History
http://www.anpa.ualr.edu/digital_library/indianvoices/
family_stories/Hill.htm

Nicholas Kristof Blog
www.nytimes.com/ontheground

Long Pross Video
http://video.nytimes.com/video/2009/01/03/
opinion/1194837193498/the-face-of-slavery.html

In My COuntry is a Problem/Borat video clip
http://www.youtube.com/watch?v=Vb3IMTJjzfo

U.S, President Barack Obama
http://www.barackobama.com/2008/02/05/remarks_of_
senator_barack_obam_46.php
 Miri ben Ari, "Symphony of Brotherhood."
http://www.youtube.com/watch?v=jfz1hJZPsxM

Goblet of Fire, Harry talks about both sides of his
character—the evil and the good. See last 3 minutes
http://www.youtube.com/watch?v=jtfeR4Sr_mo

Edward R. Murrow, the CBS reporter, gave the American
radio audience a stunning matter-of-fact description of
Buchenwald
http://www.youtube.com/watch?v=wYVn0hzcSs0

**Remedy of Wu Tang Clan, said it best in his song,
"Never Again."**
http://www.youtube.com/watch?v=yDxn7uolH7k

About Darfur
http://www.savedarfur.org

Raoul Wallenberg
http://www.ushmm.org/wlc/article.
php?ModuleId=10005211

The Eichmann Trial
http://www.archive.org/details/1961-04-13_Eichmann_
trial

**FACTS ABOUT THE USES OF MUSIC AS
PROPAGANDA**
http://www.freemuse.org

Movie about Righteous Gentiles:
Hiding and Seeking, a film by Menachem Daum
http://www.beliefnet.com/Faiths/Judaism/2005/09/
God-Is-The-Director.aspx

*L*ove and kindness are the very basis of society. If we lose these feelings, society will face tremen-dous difficulties; the survival of humanity will be endangered.

The Dalai Lama

Index

Symbols

9/11 62

A

Abadi, Moussa 99-100
Abel 21, 23, 52
About Darfur 234
Abrahamic faiths 130
Abu Ghraib Prison 33
Actors Studio 86
Adam and Eve 19-21
Africa 43, 80
African Anime Black Muslims 5
African Christians 88
African Muslims 155
Agence France-Presse 13
Agent Orange 62
Ahmadinejad, Mahmoud 13, 69, 134
AIDS 9, 77, 80
Aktion Reinhard 178
Alabama 40
Albania 91
Albanians 53, 54
al-Husayni, Mohammad Amin 177
Allach 151
Allies 178
Al Qaeda 133
Alsace, France 150
America 39, 61, 68, 79, 87, 94
American Army 151
American concentration camp 42
American Gathering of Jewish Holocaust Survivors and
        Their Descendants 103
American Jewish community 176
American libel laws 124
American Zone in Germany 112
Anti-Defamation League 228
antisemitic 177

I

J

M

O

P

ABOUT THE AUTHORS

Jeanette Friedman, a daughter of Holocaust survivors, founded the first Second Generation group in New Jersey in December 1979. She served as Second Generation Education Liaison to the United States Holocaust Memorial Council and on N.J. Governor Tom Kean's Holocaust Education Commission in the early 1980s. She also served as the Education Coordinator for The International Network of Children of Jewish Holocaust Survivors. In 1983, she was appointed to The Goldberg Commission to Examine the Role of American Jews During the Holocaust.

Today Ms. Friedman, a freelance journalist, editor and public speaker, is the CEO and editor-in-chief of The Wordsmithy, a publishing company she founded in 1985. The company specializes in books related to Holocaust history, Judaism and survivor memoirs. She is also Communications Director of the American Gathering of Jewish Holocaust Survivors and Their Descendants.

David Gold is the eldest son of Holocaust survivors. He is currently the Managing Director of Strategic Capital Advisors, LLC. He is a former lecturer and member of the faculty at Brooklyn College in the Judaic Studies Department and the Hebrew Union College. He served as Director of the National Commission on Youth for the American Jewish Congress, was a founding Director of The American Endowment School in Budapest, Hungary, and served on the board of the Endowment for Democracy in Eastern Europe. He is also a Council member of the American Gathering of Jewish Holocaust Survivors and Their Descendants.

He was appointed to the Vietnam Memorial Commission of the City of New York by Mayor Koch. The Public Advocate of the City Of New York has issued a proclamation recognizing his contributions to the community.